D1359473

Teachings of Jesus

IN MATTHEW 5-7

Teachings of Jesus

IN MATTHEW 5-7

H. Leo Eddleman

Convention Press

Nashville, Tennessee

Printed in the United States of America
250. JUL 55 R.R.D.

About the Author

Dr. H. Leo Eddleman is a native Mississippian, born April 4, 1911. Receiving his high-school education in Mississippi, he completed the Bachelor of Arts degree at Mississippi college. Dr. Eddleman attended the Southern Baptist Theological Seminary in Louisville, Kentucky, where he earned the Master of Theology and Doctor of Philosophy degrees.

This book, *Teachings of Jesus in Matthew 5-7*, grows out of a rich background of personal study and varied experience in denominational service. Dr. Eddleman served one term as a foreign missionary from 1936 through 1941, including two years at Jerusalem, one year at Tel Aviv, and three years at Nazareth. He served as professor of Semitic Languages at New Orleans Baptist Theological Seminary, 1941-42; as pastor of Parkland Baptist Church, Louisville, Kentucky, 1942-52; and as professor of Old Testament and Hebrew at the Southern Baptist Theological Seminary, 1950-54.

Dr. Eddleman has been president of Georgetown College, Georgetown, Kentucky, since June 1, 1954. He and Mrs. Eddleman have two daughters, Sarah and Evelyn.

The Sunday School Training Course

THE Sunday School Training Course prepared by the Sunday School Department of the Baptist Sunday School Board is one of the major means of promoting Sunday school work. Its influence is limited only by its use.

The six sections of the course include studies in Bible, doctrines, evangelism, Sunday school leadership and administration, teaching, age group studies, and special studies. The range of the course is broad, for the field of Sunday school work is broad and requires comprehensive and specific training. Sixteen books are required for the completion of each diploma.

The study of the training course is not to be limited to the present Sunday school workers. Most churches need twice as many workers as are now enlisted. This need can be supplied by training additional workers now. Members of the Young People's and Adult classes and older Intermediates should be led to study these books, for thereby will their service be assured. Parents will find help as they study what the Sunday school is trying to do.

SPECIAL NOTE TO INSTRUCTORS:

During your teaching of this book will you check with the Sunday school superintendent and see if an accurate record of training for the workers is kept. If not, please urge him to set up such a file with an associate superintendent of training in charge. File cards for this purpose may be ordered at nominal cost from your nearest Baptist Book Store.

A. V. WASHBURN

Secretary, Teaching and Training
Sunday School Department
Baptist Sunday School Board

Contents

Teachings of Jesus

IN MATTHEW 5-7

1

The Upward Way

MATTHEW 5:1–2, 48; 7:28–29

CHRISTIANITY has not been tried and found wanting. It has been tried and found difficult, and consequently many have ceased trying.

But one glance at a life like that of Lottie Moon, John Milton, or Albert Schweitzer makes one want to keep on trying. The very memory of John Bunyan, George Truett, or Charles Spurgeon stimulates desire to walk in Christ's way.

I. THE UPWARD WAY (MATT. 5:1–2)

On seeing the multitudes Jesus "went up into a mountain" and taught. The Sermon (Teaching) on the Mount has ever since remained a formula for lifting Christians to higher ground. Its message bears all the marks of coming from above. Whether Christ delivered it from a peak with people sitting on the sloping ground before him or on a level place near the top as Luke implies in the word "plain" (Luke 6:17), this sermon comes from a high level—both figuratively and literally. It calls for the highest in ethics and the best in conduct.

No mere man could or would have formulated such principles. The first time you *read* them you feel sure they will not work; the first time you *try* them you know nothing else will work. They call for perfection in yourself but demand that you make allowance for imperfection in others. To read

1

them creates a holy ambition to walk the upward way and
should inspire us to sing:

> I want to scale the utmost height,
>   And catch a gleam of glory bright;
> But still I'll pray 'til *life* I've found,
>   "Lord, lead me on to higher ground."

JOHNSON OATMAN, JR.

Jesus gave these teachings primarily to those called "disciples," or "learners." Now there can be devotion without
learning, but there cannot be much development. Church
members are admittedly inconsistent or weak sometimes, but
true disciples have committed themselves to keep on learning to be better. They do not claim to be perfect men—they
are imperfect men following a perfect Saviour.

1. *The Multitudes* (*Matt. 5:1*)

It was on "seeing the multitudes" that Jesus went up into
the mountain to deliver these teachings. The sight of the
multitudes always moved him to compassion. The masses of
struggling, tired, suffering, frustrated human beings touched
the deepest recesses of his heart. And he could not see them
without doing something to better their plight.

The Temple services as then held did little to meet the real
needs of the people. The priests were satisfied as long as they
maintained the ritual and the people attended the ceremonies of bloody animal sacrifices. Nothing should stop that; it
was their religion. Not even a robbed and bleeding Jew lying
in the ditch could deter priest or Levite in his haste to get
to his perfunctory routine! Jesus praised the Samaritan who
suspended all other duties until he had met the needs of the
hapless victim of man's cruelty. After healing their bodies
and relieving their distress (Matt. 4:24–25), Jesus proceeded
to teach the people about right living, reverence, judgment,

salvation—the best proof of the genuineness of his concern for them.

"That government *of* the people, *by* the people, and *for* the people should not perish from the earth," concluded a Fourth of July orator, only to have an elderly soldier in blue interrupt with a cracked voice, "Mr. Lincoln didn't say that. I was there and heard him. He said: 'that government of the *people*, by the *people*, for the *people* might not perish from the earth.'"

It is the needs of the *people* which should determine the nature of the Christian's actions and the direction of the church's efforts.

The next step for evangelistic, church-minded Christians is the "Teaching" on the Mount. It supplies the pattern for the changed life of repentance (*metanoia*)—the theme of the preaching of both Jesus and John the Baptist. Having demanded *metanoia*-living as indispensable to discipleship, Jesus proceeded to teach the pattern of conduct by which man can realize it.

2. *The Teacher-King* (*Matt. 5:2*)

The disciples called Jesus "Teacher" or Master more than by any other title. Having trusted him as Saviour, let us now make him "Master." Having received him as Redeemer, let us now hear him as Teacher.

> Hushed be the noise and the strife of schools,
> Volume and pamphlet, sermon and speech,
> The lips of the wise and the prattle of fools,
> Let the Son of man teach.
>
> Who has the key to the future but He?
> Who can unravel the knots of the skein?
> We have groaned and have travailed
> and sought to be free.
> We have travailed in vain.

> Bewildered, dejected and prone to despair,
>   To Him, as at first, do we turn and beseech.
> Our ears are all open, give heed to our prayer,
>   O Son of Man, teach.[1]
>   —AUTHOR UNKNOWN

This Teacher was different. He illustrated his teachings with a perfect life. His tone of authority was penetrating. It made the content of his teaching seem new. He called for a new order made of new men living by new principles—not ephemeral idealism for a remote golden age but realism for the pressures and tensions of life's present complicated relationships. Matthew emphasized the messianic and kingly nature of this Saviour-Teacher. But never was there a king so concerned for the well-being of his subjects. The character Jesus inspires in men makes it impossible for them to remain indefinitely in the gloom of a world stalemated in sin.

II. THE THEME OF THE TEACHING ON THE MOUNT (MATT. 5:48)

"Be ye therefore perfect, even as your Father which is in heaven is perfect" (Matt. 5:48). This verse, like a stackpole for the rest of the teaching, comes at about the halfway point. Jesus did not teach on a large number of different subjects; rather did he apply the one subject of right living to so many different life activities that it pointed to "perfection." It is a difficult word; but Jesus used it and we must therefore face it frankly.

1. *A Neglected Ideal*

The usual approach is to explain that the Bible does not call for "absolute perfection." Frequently this is done in such a way as to eliminate the urgency of the command. But this

---

[1] Truett, George, *A Quest for Souls* (Nashville: Broadman Press, 1917), p. 109.

is not "doctrinal teaching," and the doctrinaire approach would tend to siphon off the high quality of life the Lord calls for in his disciples. This sermon, as a royal "manifesto" early enunciating the characteristics and behavior of the subjects of the King, touches practically every note on the keyboard of morality and ethics.

Even trial and testing come to the Christian "that ye may be perfect and entire, lacking in nothing" (James 1:4 ASV). There is a sense in which Christians are called on to be "perfect." This is the ultimate goal of faith and Christian discipleship. Anything less is sin. Paul prayed and preached so as to "present every man perfect in Christ" (Col. 1:28; 2 Cor. 13:9). We should be surprised if the perfect Saviour representing the holy God had set anything less as the objective of his followers. "Be ye therefore perfect . . ." It is like an obedient lad heeding his father's request to bring a glass of water, though smudgy fingers cause a brown trickle down the outer edge of the glass. So we can love wholeheartedly and enthusiastically, but ever with the imprint of our imperfection in sight.

Because of the almost fanatical interpretations of "perfection" we have often recoiled from the Lord's command. But we must face it in courage and humility: Jesus expects us to strive for perfection. A low aim will almost certainly mean a low mark. The higher the goal, the loftier the final achievement. Ideals are like stars; ancient mariners could never reach up and touch them, but by keeping their eyes on them, they guided their ships safely! We have derived entirely too much comfort from the fact that "perfection" does not mean sinless perfection. "Be ye therefore perfect." This is the goal and anything less is not enough.

An incident related by William L. Stidger points up this truth:

My friend Dr. Ezra Cox, who works in home missions, spent several weeks recently among the Southern Negroes of the Methodist Church. He was accompanied by a famous Negro bishop on his rounds of preaching to the responsive Negroes.

One morning as the bishop was preaching a fervent sermon, an old mammy got up from her seat and started to dance up and down the aisle of the church. The bishop, evidently accustomed to such procedure, went on with his sermon as if nothing were happening.

After the sermon, Dr. Cox said to the woman, "Why did you get to dancing this morning when the bishop was preaching?"

Said the old mammy, "I tell you, frien', when I gets religion it makes de bottom o' my feet tickle and itch, and I jest gotta dance to 'spress myself. I jest gotta dance fo' de Lawd God Almighty!"

That evening the bishop took ill; Dr. Cox had to do the preaching. Just when he got well started he saw that same woman in his congregation, and he wondered if he would stir her into a dancing mood with his sermon as the bishop had done in the morning.

He preached his most fervent sermon and kept watching her, but she did no dancing that night. In fact, while she seemed to be listening intently, she did not move from her seat. He was discouraged, for he felt that his sermon must be a failure. He was talking about giving to missions, giving to help other people poorer than they were. But his words seemed to be falling on hard and stony ground as far as that woman was concerned. The preacher was disappointed.

Then suddenly toward the end of his sermon he noticed that old mammy begin to sway back and forth on her seat. Her eyes shone with fire. Sweet and low she began to sing an old Negro spiritual, which went in its chorus something like this:

> "Lord, we gotta give one hundred per cent;
> Ninety-nine and a half won't do;
> Lord, we gotta give one hundred per cent,
> Ninety-nine and a half won't do."

She had hardly started when the whole church took up the refrain:

> "Lord, we gotta give one hundred per cent;
> Ninety-nine and a half won't do."

He stopped his sermon to listen and then heard her improvise this phrase:

"I wanna tell Moses, I wanna tell Moses dat
We gotta give one hundred per cent;
Ninety-nine and a half won't do!"

Each stanza started off with the names of some Biblical character, "I wanna tell Moses, . . . I wanna tell Isaiah, . . . I wanna tell Amos, . . . I wanna tell John, . . . I wanna tell Jesus dat . . . Ninety-nine and a half won't do!"

It was a stirring experience to hear that response to his challenge; and it was thrilling to me to see how it links up with our needs now. We can't get by with halfhearted giving of our money, our time, our labor, our loyalty.

"We gotta give one hundred per cent;
Ninety-nine and a half won't do!" [2]

Our philosophy of "perfect living" has sometimes been like the implied attitude of American leaders in 1933: Since we could not have absolute and unanimous abstinence from alcoholic beverages, abstinence must be wrong altogether. Let us therefore reverse the policy and see how many Americans we can induce to become drinkers! And so the campaign to make all America a drinking nation goes on apace. Because we cannot achieve absolute perfection is no justification for ignoring the Lord's command to strive to be as nearly perfect as possible.

2. *Meaning of Perfection*

God described Job as a man that was "perfect and upright, and one that feared God, and turned away from evil" (Job 1:1 ASV). Throughout the Bible, "perfection" often means fulness, completeness, or sufficiency.

"Six daughters were born in succession to an Arab family in the Lebanon Mountains (northern section of old Palestine). Giving them symbolic names according to custom, the Arab father named the seventh one 'Tamama,' and by request told our missionary that when the seventh child came

---

[2] From *More Sermons in Stories* by William L. Stidger. Copyright 1944 by Whitmore & Stone. By permission of Abingdon Press.

and there was still no boy, it was time to use a name indicating 'sufficiency, enough, complete!' 'Tamama' is the very word used in the Bible to describe Job as 'perfect'." [3]

Thus it is perfection in the sense of mature, fully developed, well rounded out for which we are to strive. The Sermon on the Mount will seem unworkable and unrealistic unless we accept this goal. When we do accept it, it will appear to be the only way for disciples of the Master-Teacher, for students of the Jesus-way, to show unabated concern for glorifying their Redeemer and striving to help make an old world new.

III. THE AUTHORITY OF JESUS (MATT. 7:28-29)

If the "Teaching" on the Mount is not true, then it does not matter whether we study it seriously. If it is true, then nothing else matters so far as our daily responsibilities are concerned. The people who first heard this teaching got the impression that it was true. They listened intently not because they were being entertained. It was not a case of "administering laughing gas for the painless extraction of sin." The authority of Jesus gripped them. "And it came to pass, when Jesus had ended these sayings, the people were astonished at his doctrine [teaching]: for he taught them as one having authority, and not as the scribes."

The scribes boasted of never giving forth a thought but that it had rabbinical precedent. Practically everything they said was a "quote." Jesus spoke in his own compelling authority, and the people somehow had to listen.

1. Christ's Authority Stems from Five Factors

(1) *Truth.*—What Jesus taught was true, and the people knew it. Truth cannot be gainsaid. If one of Jesus' sayings

---

[3] Eddleman, H. Leo, *To Make Men Free* (Nashville: Broadman Press, 1954), pp. 34–35.

could be demonstrated to be untrue, his authority to command us would be dissolved. Modern psychology and psychiatry are largely a rehashing of many truths and principles set forth by Christ.

(2) *Compassion.*—Jesus' teachings are helpful. He never did or taught one thing that hurt anybody. If one of his principles could be shown to be detrimental to mankind, then it would diminish his authority by that much. There is something indescribably compelling about One whose every deed and utterance benefits.

(3) *Practicability.*—Jesus' teachings actually work. No matter how loving, how true the teacher, if his principles are unworkable, he cannot hold us. In much that he taught, Jesus' head appeared to be in the clouds, but his feet were always on the ground. Much of the workable psychology, economics, and sociology of the twentieth century is but a reversion to principles Christ enunciated clearly nineteen hundred years ago.

At the close of World War I a soap manufacturer walking down a street with his pastor was bemoaning the "failure" of Christianity. "After nineteen centuries of preaching and teaching Christ, there is still so much evil in the world, I don't see how you can go on preaching the gospel."

"I don't see how you can go on manufacturing soap," retorted the pastor. "Look at that little urchin playing in the gutter. Neck and ears filthy. There's still so much dirt in the world. Soap is such a failure."

"But" countered the soap manufacturer, "If people will just apply the soap, they'll be clean."

"Yes," concluded the pastor, "and if men will but apply Christ to their daily living, they will be clean."

(4) *Judgment.*—The authority of Jesus lies ultimately in the fact that he is Judge. Whether what he says is helpful, pleasant, or otherwise, he is our Creator and will one day judge us. Today he would save us and teach us to live nobly

(John 3:17). Tomorrow we shall stand before him in judgment (2 Cor. 5:10) and, "Every tree that bringeth not forth good fruit is hewn down, and cast into the fire'" (Matt. 7:19).

A well-dressed man stopped to help a tourist with a flat tire. Some weeks later the latter was hailed into court on a serious charge. The judge trying his case was the man who had been kind to him on the road.

"I am glad you know me already, Judge; you'll surely be lenient," exclaimed the tourist.

In giving a stiff sentence the judge said firmly, "I was your benefactor yesterday; I am your judge today."

Christ would be our Helper and Saviour before becoming our Judge.

We readily accede to the statement that there is an element of the arbitrary in the authority of Christ. Obedience to him is not optional, it is obligatory. Society cannot exist without duly constituted authority at proper levels.

All true authority stems from God. Heaven's authority permits governments as "ordained of God" (Rom. 13:1). The governmental authority permits a system conducive to proper authority in school and home. Respect for authority must begin at the grass-roots level—in the home. Disrespect for law and the rights of others on the part of teen-agers reflects failure of parents to inculcate respect for parental authority.

When a child first attempts to thwart the parental will, then is the time to establish control and teach respect for law. The child who gets his way from the beginning is a potential delinquent.

We should explain the reason for law and obedience; arbitrariness is highly undesirable. But there are times when obedience is to be expected regardless. The immature cannot always apprehend the reason behind certain rules. They are to obey them anyhow.

A fourteen-year-old daughter in a northwestern community became tired of Training Union. She announced her decision not to attend it or its annual summer encampment any more. Distracted parents expressed their regrets and apologies to the pastor. The following Sunday the pastor read a statement as part of his sermon so he could not be misquoted: "I expect my children to conform to the standards of our home as long as they are sufficiently immature for me to support them. That means they will participate in family prayer, attend Training Union, Sunday school, and worship, take what trips to encampments and assemblies we deem best. We try to explain carefully the good reasons behind our family ideals and customs. When they accept them, so much the better. When they fail to, they are going to conform to them anyhow and respect the authority of this home."

That night the teen-ager was in Training Union. She attended the summer encampment later and has since become a charming volunteer for full-time Christian service.

Some few children, after being compelled to attend religious meetings, rebel from them completely in later life. In one community alone there are three preachers' sons who use this flimsy excuse for their secularistic, irreligious living. But for every case like this, there are thousands of devout Christian men and women who owe their faith to the framework of authority within which their parents reared them. Respect for the authority of Christ, the King of kings, begets respect for all proper authority! Spiritual anarchy is the seedbed of political anarchy, communism, delinquency, immorality, and the breakup of the home.

(5) *His own person.*—Christ never prefaced his teaching with "Thus saith the Lord." The prophets did; and the scribes quoted the prophets as their authority. Christ's authority depended not upon "external credentials" but upon himself. "Ye have heard that it was said by them of old

time, . . . but I say unto you" (Matt. 5:27–28). "Heaven and earth shall pass away: but my words shall not pass away" (Luke 21:33; Matt. 5:18). Thus he made his words equal in authority to the law.

Jesus demonstrated his authority over nature (Luke 8: 24), disease (Luke 8:48), demons (Mark 5:13), and death (Luke 7:14–17).

He demonstrated his authority by assuming the prerogatives of deity, including that of forgiving sins (Mark 2:1–12).

Jesus had authority for abolishing or changing religious forms. "The Son of man is lord even of the sabbath" (Mark 2:28 ASV). It is not surprising therefore that the Lord rose on the "first day of the week" (our Sunday, Luke 24:1); that the first purely "Christ-ian" services were on Sunday evenings (the first day of the week) with the Lord present (John 20:19); that the apostles, filled with the Holy Spirit from the day of Pentecost, were led early to conduct services on the "first day of the week" to break bread in worship (Acts 20:7); that commandment concerning the time for giving designated "the first day of the week" (1 Cor. 16:2); and that as a climax of Jesus' lordship over the day set apart for worship his followers later called it, not sabbath but, "the Lord's day" (Rev. 1:10). He is indeed "Lord of the sabbath." He changed it from Saturday to Sunday, and only by an inexplicable if not satanic determination to revert to Judaism could one repudiate the Lord's authority on the question.

Jesus demonstrated his unique authority over men. "Follow me," he commanded, and men of all walks did so. Without breaking their wills, Jesus imposed his own will on men and became the highest authority for them. Those who themselves were versed in matters involving authority recognized Jesus' unique status among men. The Roman centurion with his military mind, in acknowledging the arbitrary power of Christ in healing, readily recognized authority for what it is:

"For I *also* am a man set under *authority,* having under me soldiers, and I say unto one, Go, and he goeth; and to another, Come, and he cometh; and to my servant, Do this, and he doeth it" [author's italics] (Luke 7:8).

2. *The Need for a Seat of Authority in Religion Is Twofold*

(1) *Authority is necessary to religious unity.*—A final court of appeal for settling all religious questions helps avoid hopeless confusion. Three efforts at such authority are familiar in one form or another to most men: "(1) the individual conscience, together with reason and experience; (2) an infallible institution, the Church, expressing itself finally through an infallible Papacy; and (3) the supreme authority of a Person, Jesus Christ, speaking through an infallible record as God's inspired revelation to men." [4]

Actually the New Testament was composed and clothed with the direct authority of the Lord Jesus Christ and that of the Holy Spirit in the apostles. The Scriptures are therefore the final authority for faith and practice in true Christianity. The disagreements in interpreting the Scriptures are negligible as compared with the contradictions of supposedly infallible men, one of whom might decree the burning of the Scriptures or those who had translated them into the language of the common people, while a successor would decree an indulgence of 400 days for reading the Scriptures for 15 minutes! [5]

(2) *Authority is necessary to the well-being of the individual.*—Man is so constituted that he needs authority in all fields. Without it he is like a powerful motor torn from its foundation, projecting its energy in an uncontrolled fashion.

A famous psychiatrist says that a chief element in the treatment of all demented people is stern authority. Most of

---

[4] Rone, Wendell Holmes, *The Baptist Faith and Roman Catholicism* (Kingsport: Kingsport Press, Inc., 1952), p. 1. Used by permission.

[5] Flyleaf of Douay Version of the Bible.

these patients are "just people who have lost control." To cure them he puts them under control like children in a nursery. Every hour of their day is mapped out in strict routine. Most of them rave rebelliously but soon learn that "father's word is law—father, in their case, being the doctors and staff—and that the law will be enforced." As they learn to discipline themselves, to recognize and control their illusions, they are cured!

Human beings under the control of Jesus Christ are cured, or, better still, his way of life becomes to them a preventive for the moral ills of the day. For normal men the framework of divine law is sufficiently large for them to exercise freedom of choice, but it is conforming to the law and authority divinely written into the structure of life and the universe which gives man his widest channel of self-expression. Only by enslaving himself to the authority of Christ can he become truly free.

Let us now submit to the Lord's authority in studying this teaching so that going from one principle to another will be a series of spiritual ascensions to the summit with him.

QUESTIONS FOR REVIEW AND EXAMINATION

1. By what title was Jesus called more than any other?
2. State the theme of the Sermon on the Mount as indicated by this book.
3. Name two of the factors on which Jesus' authority is based.

FOR FURTHER STUDY

1. List some of the religious bodies which proclaim the doctrine of "sinless perfection" and analyze their teachings from at least two of their textbooks.
2. Using a concordance, trace the word "authority" in the Four Gospels wherever it is related to Jesus.

2

The New Manhood

MATTHEW 5:3-12

THE LAW began with a curse. Ever it held a threat over the people for the least violation and stimulated fear and trembling.

The gospel of the kingdom begins with "blessedness" or happiness. The center of gravity of the King's subjects is in the moral realm, and no distortion of things physical can upset them. Like a gyroscope they retain an inward balance regardless of outward circumstances—a new type of manhood!

I. DISCIPLES ARE HAPPY (MATT. 5:3-12)

The Beatitudes show how happiness is possible to those who ordinarily are not expected to be happy. The poor, the mournful, the meek—these are the happy ones in Christ's kingdom. Their happiness depends, however, not on something they do or get, but on what they are in themselves. It is their character or inner state of being which is the cause of their joy.

In addition, each character quality is assured a specially adapted reward. These rewards are primarily for the present life, but they also span the distance from earth to heaven. Each of the nine Beatitudes (from Latin *beatus*, meaning blessed or happy) has three parts: a statement of the happiness, the character, and the particular reward for each case. The ancient Hebrew form for "blessed" in Psalm 1:1, from which it comes, is literally, "O the happinesses of." This plural suggests an abundance of joy.

Joy is a Christian distinctive. It was in the joy of the Holy Spirit that both Christ and the early disciples lived and moved. The gospel is never a "joy-killer." Anything a Christian is asked to give up is something he never should have had in the first place. Christ never takes without returning something better. The ancient catechism has it right: "The chief end of man is to know the Lord and enjoy him forever."

Whenever religion does not bring abiding joy and happiness, there is something wrong with that religion—or with the man who has it. Many religions admittedly bring not joy but fear. A "works-salvation" can only result in doubt and insecurity, leaving one to worry whether he has "worked enough" to make it.

Sometimes the problem lies in the believer, even though he professes a Bible faith. He may not be growing in the knowledge of the Lord. He may not be studying the Word reverently and regularly. Many fail to enjoy the Bible, not because it contradicts itself, but because it contradicts their conduct.

Some Christians have just enough religion to make them miserable. They have enough to keep them from going to a night club or dance on Wednesday night but not quite enough to make them get up and go on to prayer meeting! Christ intends for his followers to be happy, but they can never be so as long as they remain in an eddy of indifference or worldliness.

Let such Christians break out of the subtle whirl into the great stream of Bible-reading, Christ-serving, church-loving Christian living, and they will know the abounding joy of their salvation at once. From attending hardly one service a week, let them try going to more. From seldom taking part in the organized work of the church and kingdom, let them lay aside a superficial dignity and carry the load of a loyal church member. From having never witnessed for the Lord, let them take a list of shut-ins or lost people and visit them earnestly.

II. The Inner Basis for Happiness and Reward
(Matt. 5:3–12)

Happiness and reward are based upon inner character qualities.

1. *The Poor in Spirit* (*Matt. 5:3*)

Being free of pride and vanity, the poor in spirit are aware of their spiritual poverty. Being conscious of it, they have a deep sense of need. This is the chief prerequisite for profound Christian experience.

Many of Jesus' hearers were literally poor. He may have mentioned physical poverty first (Luke 6:20). The Roman Empire denied the poor many privileges. In Christ's kingdom they almost have a priority. Preaching the gospel to the poor was a primary function of the King-Messiah (Luke 4:18). Millions are still so poor that the only "blessedness" they can ever experience in this life is the hope that in the next life a merciful God will reward their loyalty with joy and security that will more than compensate for what they have been denied here. "For I reckon that the sufferings of this present time are not worthy to be compared with the glory which shall be revealed in us" (Rom. 8:18).

Christians have a threefold obligation to the poor: (1) to feed them (neglect here is like denying the faith; Matt. 25:41–42); (2) to preach the gospel to them; and (3) to extend them fellowship. Woe unto the church in which the poor are not welcome (James 2:1–6).

The needs and wants of the poor man practically coincide because the pangs of hunger and cold do not permit him to think far beyond his basic necessities. Thus the "poor in spirit" are those who realize their true needs. They have given up desire for things harmful and superficial. By the world's standards they do not appear to want much, while actually they long for spiritual values like kindness, honesty, forgiveness, and salvation.

Thus material poverty was so prevalent it made a graphic analogy for spiritual poverty in the eyes of Christ's hearers. A man "poor in spirit" is the opposite to the one of vaulting ambition for worldly achievement. He is the opposite of the man who pursues vain and superficial values, so called. His poverty intensifies his awareness of what is truly valuable. The poor man will work conscientiously all day long for the sure wages of a loaf of bread; his opposite may gamble away his chances for a gold mine or an oil field. The poor in spirit readily distinguish between what they want and what they need.

2. *They That Mourn* (*Matt. 5:4*)

Christ comforts every sincere mourner. Whatever the cause of sorrow, he has already anticipated it. Because of his perfect humanity he has been touched with our infirmities and feels with us. Thus the gospel is designed "to comfort the afflicted—and to afflict the comfortable."

The context obviously calls for more than ordinary mourning. It includes not only the brokenhearted, but also the contrite of spirit. Sorrow for sin and sadness because of spiritual weakness are causes for more intense mourning than death and sickness. "A broken and a contrite heart, O God, thou wilt not despise" (Psalm 51:17).

But true mourning is not so much an act as an attitude. Paid mourners used to put on quite a display of grief at the graveside. The genuine mourner might not shed a tear but be crushed within. So this "blessedness" in Christ's kingdom is dependent on qualities of *being* instead of *doing* and *having*.

3. *The Meek* (*Matt.* 5:5)

The meek are submissive to the reign of the King and the laws of his kingdom. This is true humility. "For God resisteth the proud, and giveth grace to the humble. Humble yourselves therefore under the mighty hand of God that he may exalt you in due time" (1 Peter 5:5-6). Being poor in spirit, the meek have cut themselves off from worldly desires. They mourn only for the comfort and sustenance of the King. Therefore they meekly submit themselves to his commands, and under his mighty hand of righteousness they inherit the earth—the very thing the rich and proud think they do!

The meek do not "grab up" the earth. They inherit it. They want only such portions of the earth as will enable them to do the will of God. "'All this is my land,' said a man to his poor cousin. 'Yes, but it is my landscape,' was the gentle reply. . . . The meek obey God, and so become a terror to tyrannies. 'Now the man Moses was very meek, above all the men which were upon the . . . earth' (Numbers 12:3), and his first recorded adult act was to kill a slave driver. The meek, asking of earth only a place in which to obey God, never assert themselves except in behalf of the oppressed." [1] The Beatitudes are really a full portrait of Christ himself!

Some commentators see by analogy in these three Beatitudes the three essential steps in salvation: (1) a sense of need, (2) sorrow for sin and spiritual decline (repentance), and (3) submissiveness to the Lord (faith).

4. *They That Hunger and Thirst After Righteousness* (*Matt.* 5:6)

Millions are on the verge of literal starvation. Countless others "crave" they know not what and flit from one attrac-

---

[1] From *Book of Mercies* by George Arthur Frantz. Copyright 1952. Used by special permission of the publishers, The Bobbs-Merrill Company, Inc.

tion to another like human butterflies feeding avidly on food
with vitamin deficiencies. Make up your mind what you
want, says the King. Be sure it is what you ought to have
and you will be filled.

Those hungry for the Lord shall not be "sent empty away"
(Luke 1:53). Focus all desire on that which is most desir-
able. "Delight thyself also in the Lord; and he shall give thee
the desires of thine heart" (Psalm 37:4). "Not by bread
alone," is the Christmas greeting emblazoned each year on
billboards by the thoughtful owner of a metropolitan bakery.

It is the "appetite for righteousness" which we must culti-
vate. We usually pursue that which we really want. A woman
was smiling while other class members complained about
the difficulty of getting to Sunday school regularly and
promptly because of household responsibilities and children.
The teacher explained that this woman regularly got break-
fast for her husband and nine boarders, prepared her three
children, and then walked seven blocks to the church carrying one child on her arm! She hungered for God's Word and
righteousness, and petty excuses seemed humorous to her.
To be sure, the assumption that spiritual hunger would be
satisfied in this manner is rash if the class does not supply a
high quality of both Christian fellowship and Bible teaching.

5. The Merciful (Matt. 5:7)

The longing for righteousness must be balanced by a heart
of mercy. This is not the only place in the Bible where God's
gifts are contingent on our attitude toward others. If we
would receive mercy, we must be merciful to others. God
will deal with us as we deal with our fellow men (Matt. 6:12;
18:21-35).

Who has not had mistreatments and then spontaneously
wondered if they were the result of his own unfair treatment
of another? God will not forgive our sins if we refuse to forgive those of another. We shall be judged as we judge. The

merciful man is happy because the memory of what God's mercy means to him makes him exult with every opportunity to pass it on to someone else. This is the Golden-Rule Christianity badly needed in a gold-seeking country. Drive a hard or unfair bargain and watch out for it to boomerang. We cannot all be mighty, but we can all be merciful—and is anything else mightier in the long run?

6. *The Pure in Heart* (*Matt. 5:8*)

The pure in heart see through earth's delusions to God himself—otherwise their *visions* will become *subdivisions*. Great inspirations die within us if we fail to see God. Righteousness and mercy combine to make possible the truly "pure in heart." These shall see God because they do hunger for righteousness. No compromisers are they; no conformers to Hollywood idealism are they!

In holding fast to their own lofty standards, the pure in heart have not lost sympathy for the benighted or weak one who does not yet measure up to them. Purity includes not only the capacity to abstain from evil, but also the grace to refrain from the self-righteous, pharisaical mentality that would excommunicate or consign to perdition those who have not yet become pure.

The pure in heart see God progressively on earth. They see him in others, in history, in the unfolding of his Word. One day they shall see him perfectly.

To see God is the supreme good of human existence. "When he shall appear, we shall be like him; for we shall see him as he is" (1 John 3:2). When Christ returns the second time, "every eye shall see him, and they also which pierced him" (Rev. 1:7). The saint will see him in salvation, the sinner in judgment. This is incentive for pure thinking, pure talking, pure living. An uncle used to say, "Son, you cannot keep the birds from flying over your head, but you can keep them from building nests in your hair."

7. *The Peacemakers* (*Matt. 5:9*)

Peacemakers are "blessed," but the very nature of their task opens to them a door of joy seldom known to others. First, they are called "the children of God" because what they are doing is so Godlike.

The Heavenly Father is the greatest peacemaker of all. His heart has known no surcease from its concern for unreconciled sinners since Adam and Eve fell in the garden of Eden. He made the first gestures toward reconciliation. Man ran. God pursued. When man becomes a peacemaker, he is doing what God does characteristically. Therefore such men shall be called children of God. They are most akin to the divine nature.

Peacemaking is no simple matter. Peace does not come cheap and easy. We must strive and plan for it. Peace is not merely the absence of a war; it is the presence of a will to get along. We must wage peace! The peacemaker watches for opportunities to keep the peace from being broken. He is a neighbor who needs no "spite fence," a friend whose tongue is not double, a mate whose disposition is not touchy, a driver whose temper is not quick-triggered in a traffic jam, a teacher patient with the slow of mind, a student forbearing toward the tedious but well-meaning lecturer. He also longs to see men at peace with God.

8. *Those Persecuted for Righteousness' Sake* (*Matt. 5:10*)

Persecution often has been the reward of him who seeks to establish the righteousness of Christ's kingdom. Not all men are sympathetic even with the righteous cause of peace. As long as there is profit in war, the human race will be subjected to intermittent blood baths. The unspiritual do not want a genuine revival to come to the nation; it would demand too much of them. There would have to be drastic changes in social, economic, and moral patterns.

Laborers want enough revival to soften capitalists; capitalists want enough to make laborers efficient. Few of us want enough to establish pure brotherhood and Christian stewardship on a worldwide basis. The world is willing to have the kind of religion that can be worn as a sort of badge of respectability but not the kind that produces *metanoia*-living (repentance).

When real religion breaks out, the world recoils or strikes back. It will not permit Christianity to touch its deeds, creeds, or supposed needs. It clings to deeds of immorality in the name of personal liberty; it waves aloft ancient creeds which were not based on the Bible in the first place; it assumes that the economy of the land is everything and that anything goes if it facilitates the making of a living. In such a world persecution is not only likely but frequent.

There is the peace *of* God as well as peace *with* God. The two go together. In the midst of persecution, even at the battle front, the Christian soldier has the promise of inner peace. Again Christ promised the kingdom of heaven. When the loss on earth is increased, the reward in heaven is greater. But notice the limitation on this promise: it is to those persecuted for righteousness' sake.

"The cause in which a man suffers is everything," a Hebrew from Belgium said. "If I remain a Jew, the anti-Semites will persecute me; if I become a Christian, my own people will persecute me. Since I must suffer either way I go, let me become a Christian and suffer for the truth."

"All that will live godly in Christ Jesus shall suffer persecution" (2 Tim. 3:12). Again it is persecution for Christ's sake. It is easy to develop a "martyr complex" and feel that every time we fail to get our way we are being persecuted. Such whining belittles church members in the eyes of the world and of one another. This Beatitude is for stout hearts and determined spirits.

A noncommissioned officer taking a military examination

wrote concerning a soldier's objective: "It is commonly supposed that a soldier's first duty is to die for his country. This is an error. His first duty is to make his enemies die for theirs!" In spiritual warfare enemies "die" when by aggressive love they are changed into friends.

Christ called for obedience to principles that could produce a new social order based on righteousness; he promised the kingdom of heaven to those who might get hurt in trying to establish it!

9. *Those Reviled Falsely for the King's Sake* (*Matt. 5:11–12*)

Unjust persecution and false accusation are an intensified form of persecution for righteousness' sake. At first this Beatitude appears to be only an extension of the preceding one, leaving eight Beatitudes instead of nine. Actually the climax of blessedness is reached in this ninth. It is more than the capacity to endure opposition to righteousness—it is the ability to rejoice even when men revile you and speak evil against you falsely for Jesus' sake.

Again the blessing depends upon the cause in which we suffer. Others often criticize us for our tactlessness, egotism, and weaknesses. This we should expect and take in stride. But if someone speaks evil against us falsely for Jesus' sake, that is, merely because we are doing his will and are identified with him—this is the severest test of all. It is "bearing his reproach" in a world that has already stigmatized pure Christianity and Christians.

To withstand such treatment puts you in good company. "Rejoice, and be exceeding glad: for great is your reward in heaven: for so persecuted they the prophets which were before you" (Matt. 5:12). Classified with the prophets! You can well afford to be exceeding glad because you still have the approval of God in heaven plus a prophet's reward. The disciples, after being imprisoned and beaten, departed "rejoicing that they were counted worthy to suffer shame for his name" (Acts 5:41). Some modern Christians have been counted that worthy in Spain, Russia—and America.

III. DISCIPLES ARE REWARDED (MATT. 5:3-12)

Following Christ always brings one immeasurable blessings and rewards.

1. *Rewards Are Appropriate*

In each case the reward is peculiarly adapted to the character quality being set forth. The reward of the *poor in spirit* is the kingdom of heaven. Their poverty is compensated for by their seeking and receiving the things of the spirit world, of character, of God himself. Those who *mourn* are comforted. The *meek,* apparently timid and pushed around by covetous worldlings, inherit the earth. The *hungry* are filled and the *merciful* obtain mercy. The *pure in heart,* undeceived by earth's mirages, see through the maze into the countenance of the Lord. *Peacemakers* take after their Progenitor and therefore they shall be called sons of God.

2. *Rewards Are Reasonable* (*Matt. 5:3*)

The word "for" begins the second half of each Beatitude. It is a forceful particle in the language of the New Testament and could be rendered "because" throughout these verses. It emphasizes the logic of what Jesus said. If a disciple denies himself, is persecuted for righteousness' sake, is reviled falsely for the Lord's sake, it is reasonable that he should be rewarded accordingly. This does not mean that God is obligated to us. In the final analysis any reward is a gift of grace to "unprofitable servants" (Luke 17:10).

Highly organized (not to say commercialized) religious systems sometimes yield to the ubiquitous urge to put heavenly rewards and salvation on a "debit and credit" basis.

This may appear to be easier than teaching Christian stewardship and may also swell the church coffers spasmodically, but it is contrary to the truth of salvation by grace and service rendered out of gratitude for what Christ did for us on Calvary's cross. The Christian must be able to view with hope, not dread, the promise, "Behold, I come quickly; and my reward is with me, to give every man according as his work shall be" (Rev. 22:12).

3. *Rewards Cover a Wide Span (Matt. 5:3, 12)*

The Christian is rewarded in this present life. He is comforted by Christ in his sorrow, and in his poverty he "inherits the earth." His hunger for righteousness is satisfied, he obtains mercy, and he is accorded the distinction of being called a son of God. Thus at least five Beatitudes point to an earthly reward.

Three Beatitudes include rewards that could be for both this life and the next (Matt. 5:3, 8, 10). "For theirs is the kingdom of heaven" means the reign of Christ in the hearts of men whether on earth or in heaven. Eternal life begins while we are yet in this present scene. Significantly the "kingdom of heaven" comes with the present tense both times (Matt. 5:3, 10). Theirs *is* the kingdom of heaven, not merely will be theirs after death. The pure in heart shall see God progressively, increasingly on earth as they grow spiritually and completely in heaven when they shall "see him as he is." "To me to live is Christ [here], . . . to die is gain [hereafter]" (Phil. 1:21).

One Beatitude (Matt. 5:12) seems to point to a reward with special reference to life after death. "For great is your reward in heaven" (Matt. 5:12). This is the climax in rewards and is linked with great joy. Those persecuted and reviled for Jesus' sake not only have a great reward in heaven, but are classified with the prophets!

Preaching on other worldly subjects is not popularly received in the twentieth century. What with our great interest in the various political philosophies of the day, we do not often ponder what is in store for us in the remote tomorrows. A man running for office is analyzed to ascertain whether he is to the "left of center" or to the "right." We must beware lest we become so preoccupied with what is "left" and what is "right" that we forget there is an "above" and a "below." There is a heaven to be gained and a hell to be missed. "Godliness is profitable for all things, having promise of the life which now is, and of that which is to come" (1 Tim. 4:8 ASV).

The profitableness of godliness reaches into two worlds: that which is and that which is to come. "My kingdom is not of this world" (John 18:36 ASV) was Christ's way of stressing that ultimately heaven is our goal, that this present scene is transitory and temporary, serving only as a training camp for our souls preparatory to eternal life with him in the great beyond. "If we have only hoped in Christ in this life, we are of all men most pitiable" (1 Cor. 15:19 ASV).

> 'Tis religion that can give
> Sweetest pleasures while we live;
> 'Tis religion must supply
> Solid comforts when we die.
>
> After death its joys will be
> Lasting as eternity;
> Be the living God my Friend,
> Then my joys shall never end!
>
> MARY MASTERS

QUESTIONS FOR REVIEW AND EXAMINATION

1. What is the meaning of "beatitude"?
2. Define either (1) the "poor in spirit" or (2) the "meek."
3. The rewards promised in the Beatitudes are to be received on earth or in heaven? Explain.

For Further Study

1. Using a standard book on mythology, describe the emphasis on happiness in the ancient cults and religions of Bible times.
2. In reading the book of Psalms through, or by means of a concordance, underscore each instance in which the word "blessed" is used in a sense similar to its use in the Beatitudes of the Sermon on the Mount.

3

The New Mission

MATTHEW 5:13-20

THE HEBREWS had lost their sense of mission. They were to be a "kingdom of priests, and a holy nation" (Ex. 19:6 ASV). All members of the Hebrew race were called to do for all the world what the priestly group did for them: stand between the people and God and bring the two together. Their quality of life was to draw all men to their God.

I. THE NEW MISSION FOR NEW MEN (MATT. 5:13-16)

The drawing quality of life is the new mission for the new men of Christ's kingdom. It is the magnetism of distinctive living and not the mere shouting of shibboleths. It is the mystery of a moral and spiritual cohesive and not the prattle of proselytism. Too much religious talk wears thin, but goodness never grows monotonous; kindness never becomes stale.

This mission is the responsibility of all Christ's followers. The priesthood as a special class was abolished at Christ's death. No New Testament church ever had the office of priest. Each Christian is a priest (Rev. 1:5). Everybody is somebody in the kingdom of Christ! Lack of something to feel important about can be one of life's greatest tragedies. The importance of the work of each Christian is stressed by means of two common objects in nature.

1. To Function as Salt (Matt. 5:13)

It is proverbial that salt preserves, flavors, and heals. It is presumptuous to assume that modern ritualistic, insipid,

29

lukewarm church life can have a similar effect on the world. Salt was of great value in Bible times. Formerly it probably was used as a medium of exchange.

Salt is potent. Jesus was not discouraged because the disciples were few in number at this time. A very small quantity of salt is powerful out of proportion to its size. A few genuine Christians are always powerful out of proportion to their number. By close contact with the decaying world, not through monastery methods, they can claim men for the kingdom. The Master's minority can always be "more than conquerors" because "one plus God" is still a majority.

Does salt in reasonable amounts preserve even pork from decay? Only so can true Christians save the world from moral putrefaction. Does salt give flavor to otherwise tasteless food? So do real Christians give flavor and meaning to life. Does salt properly applied heal and sustain life? So do sincere Christians properly functioning as individuals in an otherwise corrupt society heal humanity of its ills.

Impotent salt is worthless. "Ye are the salt of the earth: but . . ." Some salt has "tuckered out." It was so weak it could not stand but "one using." Or it got wet and its essence evaporated. For whatever cause, it has "lost its savour." It has become impotent and insipid. It cannot stave off the rotting process in meat nor give taste to so much as a boiled egg. It is good for nothing—but to be cast out. This is sharp language, but the analogy is clear. When a church member no longer lives right, no longer witnesses, no longer lives so as to promote Christ's kingdom, the church is better off without him.

The salt of the Dead Sea for centuries was worthless until modern science learned to separate it and combine it with other valuable elements. Today dredge boats of a multi-million-dollar chemical project ply the waters to the profit of many. So also through Christ erstwhile morally defeated men, worthless to God and humanity, are subjected to a divine alchemy that restores and renews both the fallen and backslidden. God's creatures become "new creatures" in Christ Jesus. He makes bad men good and good men better.

2. To Radiate as Light (Matt. 5:14–16)

Traveling 186,000 miles per second, light from the sun is even more indispensable to life on earth than salt. The present universal scheme of things cannot operate without sunlight. In the Scriptures light symbolizes two things: truth and righteousness—just as its opposite, darkness, is a figure of ignorance and sin. The world needs Christians who glow with the true light.

Light warms as it radiates. Its life-giving quality sustains us physically on the earth. "In him was life; and the life was the light of men" (John 1:4). The light of God's love, warm and life-giving, is the source of all religion that is not counterfeit. The word "light" in New Testament language is the root for our word "phosphorescent"; there is a continual glow.

Only Christ can say, "I am the light of the world." He is very light of very light. But he also said, "Ye are the light of the world." He is the source of light; we are reflectors. He is the sun; we are his luminaries, "satellites of the Saviour," for they that turn many to righteousness shall shine as the stars of the firmament forever (Dan. 12:3).

If we catch our light from him, are lighted within by him, we cannot help but glow. Such luminous Christianity does not come from external striving but from inner experience, inner victory over sin and self, the enthronement of Christ within the inner citadel of the soul.

The light from a disciple diffuses over an ever-widening area. The illumination is reflected first from an *individual* (v. 16), next it is in a *house* (v. 15), then a *city* (vv. 14ff), and finally it is the light of the *world* (v. 14a). The house is the first place in which the individual is to shine. If the light of love and kindness does not radiate from him at home, little good will it do the city or world!

By its very nature light shines, witnesses to its origin. Only an artificial impediment or vicious obstruction reduces or destroys it. A city set on a hill cannot be hid. Its glowing lights tell that people, life, activity are there. The purpose of lighting a candle was that it might give light. Therefore it was not put under a bushel but on a stand so that its light could benefit all in the house.

In a world dark with communism and perverted forms of religion, nothing is so helpful as the light of pure Christian living. Christians should seek to light up this world. Cheap Christianity will not do it. The "bushel" was used in business for measuring. Does preoccupation with business today put out the light of American Christians?

Years ago some bystanders mocked a Chinese Communist about to be executed. Just before the fatal shot rang out he cried, "Yes, but I'm dying for a cause; what are you living for?" While Communists are dying for communism many Christians do not seem to know what they are supposed to be living for!

False modesty puts out some lights. Men can be so robust in almost anything they do—except their service to Christ. Women can be so charming in the use of their remarkable talents in secular organizations—then become strangely shy and inept in the house of God. "First-rate loyalties to second-rate causes" may well be the divine Coroner's report on the death of mighty America someday.

Let your light so shine, Christian! "So" means you should act like a light. "Shine" in New Testament language is the very word from which we get our word "lamp." Men are supposed to see your good works and glorify your Heavenly Father because of them. What you do, do in his name. What you give, give in his name—to and through his church for the welfare of humanity.

3. *To Combine Both Qualities*

Light and salt! Such Christian qualities could save the world today—but not if kept in that order. Salt comes first, and Christians must become salt before they can perform as light. If there is too much false modesty in some areas, there is too much pride and self-seeking in others. America's worst "ism" is not communism, socialism, or political ecclesiasticism but egotism—in Christians who are supposed to be meek and poor in spirit!

Salt can preserve or heal only by losing its own identity. It must get down into direct contact with that which it would save from putrefaction. It does not perform on the stage, but out where there is flesh and blood. The Christian must first be willing to get next to sinning, suffering humanity. It is the personal touch. It is the close-up contact with the unlovely and unlovable. Light, on the contrary, must be seen. It does its work from the pedestal. A Christian must be willing to do the menial work of salt before he can qualify to perform as light.

Too many are ready to be put "up front" where they can "shine" but are not willing to go personally on a rescue mission to lost and morally decaying men. Some preachers readily shine from the pulpit on Sunday—but seldom find their way into repulsive crevices where salt is needed between Sundays. Some Sunday school and Training Union workers "preside" or teach to the point of scintillation—then procrastinate to the point of stultification about the visitation program.

He who would shine as the light of the world must first become the salt of the earth. So much more could be accomplished in Christ's kingdom, if we did not care who gets the credit! From one standpoint the disciple must not be conspicuous; from another he cannot be hidden if he would be Christian.

The central message in these verses about salt and light is the divine mission for men. The universe is characterized throughout by the principle of teleology and usefulness. There is a good purpose for all things.

A youth questioned the value of snakes until he saw his grandfather toss one into the corn crib one day and then walk away exclaiming, "There, we shall soon be rid of the rodents."

Another questioned the use of cactus plants. Then he read of a lost traveler in a desert getting enough liquid out of huge cactus leaves to slake his thirst and restore his strength sufficiently to enable him to find his way back to civilization. If God's plan admits an occasional place of such usefulness to snakes and thorny cactus leaves, how much more does it have a divine mission for men created in his image?

Some are called to "full-time" Christian service and become effective teachers, preachers, and missionaries. All Christians are called to "full-time" Christian service in another sense. Several boys in a Royal Ambassador encampment (men can seldom do better in the kingdom than lead effectively a group of boys in a chapter of this organization) had come forward in response to an invitation to yield themselves to foreign mission work if God were calling them.

Suddenly a husky youth broke into the aisle and on reaching the speaker asked to say a word. "I'm not called to be a preacher or missionary," said he. "I'm going to be a doctor right here in America. But I want to dedicate my life to be a *Christian* doctor and pledge to do all I can to help support these who have said they are going to be missionaries. I'm matching their lives with mine for Christ."

Jesus said, "Come ye after me, and I will make you to become . . ." (Mark 1:17). All disciples can "become" something by following the Master closely. An old book by the title *Glory in the Commonplace* magnifies this truth. The humblest Christian can be salt and light wherever he is, at home or abroad. When Americans travel abroad their Christian witness—or lack of it—can be so telling.

An old Negro working in the engine room of a Great Lakes steamer was heard singing:

> "Oh, you gotta get a glory
> In the work you do;
> A Hallelujah Chorus
> In the heart of you.

> "Paint, or tell a story,
> Sing, or shovel coal;
> But you gotta get a glory
> Or the job lacks soul."

The old Negro found a way to make coal-shoveling a glorious work. The glory of God in the Bible means the revelation of God's character. The simplehearted old man found that God could be revealed in the way coal was handled.

We have to get a glory in the work we do.

It has been computed that the average married woman will have to wash three hundred and forty tons of dirty dishes in her lifetime—three-million dishes. She needs to get a glory in the work she does. The average man will work one hundred thousand hours before he retires on his pension. This counts up to six-million minutes. A little glory in each of those minutes adds up to a radiant life.[1]

"And whatsoever ye do in word or deed, do all in the name of the Lord Jesus, giving thanks to God and the Father by him" (Col. 3:17). This is the way to get a glory in the work we do.

II. THE NEW MEANING TO HISTORY (MATT. 5:17-20)

Many Hebrews recoiled from Jesus because they thought the new wine of his kingdom would destroy the old wine-

---

[1] From *Book of Mercies* by George Arthur Frantz. Copyright 1952. Used by special permission of the publishers, The Bobbs-Merrill Company, Inc.

skins of their religious forms. He stated forthrightly early in his ministry that he came not to destroy the law and prophets but to fulfil. The law was to bless all men morally and spiritually. The glamor of the external expressions of the law had blinded the Hebrews to its real purpose. If they would move on to perfection, they must learn to distinguish between the shell and the kernel.

1. *Jesus and the Past* (*Matt. 5:17*)

It is natural to fear the loss of the heritage projected to us out of the past. The apparently new in Christ and his kingdom charter frightened the Jews. They wanted to keep what they had. "The grip of the customary" had them.

According to popular thought, the coming of King-Messiah's reign was to bring political revolution. This might even lead to the abolishing of cherished institutions and the casting off of moral restraints. Hence their question, What is the relation of this new order to past history?

The process of divine revelation bears the marks of progress, reaching its culmination in Jesus Christ. He is the apex of the pyramid of revelation. Christianity is the flower of which Judaism is the bud. What the Jews—and some Christians—fail to grasp is that pure Judaism is embryonic Christianity and genuine Christianity is Judaism full-grown. The coming of Christ's kingdom is the consummation of God's self-disclosure begun in the Old Testament.

History is a unity. God moves in the onflowing stream of human events toward a well-defined objective. The British historian, Toynbee, sees in history only a "succession of civilizations," and some question whether he recognizes any continuity and purpose therein. History is more than a record of all human events up to the present; it is a written record of the remembered past.

It is more than passing strange that the best-remembered portions of history were the first to be printed: the Bible and its telescopic view of the past. The father of history was not Herodotus but the author of 1 and 2 Samuel, who anticipated him by several centuries. Three things he did for which we are indebted: (1) recorded the past with reliability; (2) laid down general rules for interpreting history; and (3) anticipated the direction of future history.

Jesus regarded his kingdom as a fulfilment or consummation of the past. The prophets foresaw and foretold; he fulfilled and "filled full." Moses and the prophets participated in his kingdom by laying foundational principles expressed in accordance with the moral and intellectual level of their day.

2. Permanence of the Law (Matt. 5:18)

The first word in verse 18 is "Amen," meaning verily or of a truth. It always introduces something of unusual import. Jesus would preserve what Moses had left the Jews. He would do more than preserve it; he would take it to its highest destiny. Heaven and earth would pass away ere the divine law would.

It was comparatively easy for Jesus to tell the Jews he had not come to destroy the law. It was not so easy to tell them that he *was* going to destroy their false conceptions of it. They thought it was largely external; he must show that it is inner and spiritual (Jer. 31:31-33). They made a nationalistic code of it; he must show its universal application. They made it a system for supporting an institution, the Temple; he must demonstrate that institutions are worthless except as they help and bless men in righteousness.

The law and the Temple were made for men and not men for them. Both Christ and the apostles would be persecuted for showing the difference between ceremonies of the law and the moral or ethical essence of it.

The law was incomplete in its Old Testament expressions. When Jeremiah prophesied a new covenant (Jer. 31:31), he automatically made the first old. Pious Jews knew there was more to come and that it would come through the Messiah. In their thinking, his political function so completely overshadowed the spiritual that few recognized him when he did come. Yet Christ is the end of the law. He both fulfils it and is its fulfilment. Even Renan said, "All history is incomprehensible without Christ."

Times change and many values are said to be relative. In human history we see how that "the middle of the road" of today would have been considered rank socialism several decades ago. Actually the 1948 platforms of both major political parties in the United States were almost literal reproductions of the 1924 platform of the socialist party. In the midst of change it is refreshing to know that God's Word is absolute.

Not a jot or tittle of the divine law will pass away until all be fulfilled. A jot is the smallest letter in the Hebrew alphabet. A tittle is also a very small stroke like an apostrophe. It is only an adjunct of a letter or a curlicue. Not even one of these "shall pass from the law, till all be fulfilled." This hyperbole means that no essential part of divine law will ever be done away with.

"For ever, O Lord, thy word is settled in heaven" (Psalm 119:89). God will not change it once it has gone forth, nor will he designate any pastor, bishop, or pope to nullify or modify his word. Whether it be what some would call the "jot" of democratic church government, the "tittle" of baptism in its proper form, or the essential and primary principle of right treatment of other races, God does not want it changed. He has not authorized anyone else to change it.

The development of spiritual values and ethical conduct is magnified in God's law. Its written expression is not marred by the marks of the imperfect hands inspired to write it. It is undiluted with erroneous teaching and false philosophies. The Egyptians had fascinating theories of evolution in vogue in Moses' day. Bible writers did not mix them into the biblical record of creation to show that they kept abreast of "modern thought." Why should they preserve those flies in amber?

"The law was our schoolmaster to bring us unto Christ" (Gal. 3:24). Its many meticulous rules had their place. They created an awareness of sin and a sense of need designed to prepare the people for the coming of Christ. Every animal sacrificed in the Temple according to commandment pointed up the heinousness of sin and opened the way for the sacrifice of the Lamb of God.

3. *The Law and Greatness* (*Matt. 5:19*)

The scribes and Pharisees would "say, and do not" (Matt. 23:3). But whosoever shall "do and teach" these least commandments shall be called great in the kingdom of heaven. The doing comes before teaching. Teachers, preachers, and churches who claim to be setting forth the "full" gospel had best make sure they are living "full" lives.

The test of greatness is not in membership rolls, financial reports, or building equipment, but in doing the will of God. A man can omit some of the teachings of Christ and "get by," but he is "least" in the kingdom of heaven.

This emphasis on keeping and teaching the "least" commandments reveals the Lord's own evaluation of the divine law in its totality. Men moving on toward perfection cannot be remiss concerning teachings which may at first blush seem unimportant. Actually no divine command is even comparatively unimportant. "Leave off the nonessential and stress only the essential parts of the Word of God" is the clamor of a generation gone delicatessen in its attitude toward doctrine. Christ had no time for "nonessentials"; if he taught them at all, they are essential.

"Least" New Testament commandments, some aver, are seen in baptism, the Lord's Supper, or church membership. But the Lord himself gave these, and to omit or change them invokes the stigma. To presume to tamper with divine law and then teach men so is partial repudiation of the kingdom charter according to which God would project his holy government.

These so-called commandments are sooner or later relevant to life and man's well-being. Pork was forbidden to Jews in the law, and now in times of modern refrigeration techniques we know why: pork spoils twice as quickly as beef and three times as readily as mutton and is more subject to disease bacteria.

It seems a small matter if one takes that "least" commandment about graven images lightly (Ex. 20:4). Are not images an "aid to worship?" it is argued. But these "aids" to worship quickly take on more meaning—to the point of superstition. The ill effect of such superstition is attested by more than one eyewitness who saw American soldiers killed and wounded by machine guns from an Italian monastery during World War II because they dared not fire on a "sacred" building which housed images of deity and saints. Suppose it had been an evangelical church! Better it had been blown to bits at once than that one American soldier be killed by Nazis and Fascists infesting its walls! The "least" commandments are not small in the final analysis.

4. *Righteousness That Exceeds* (*Matt. 5:20*)

The scribes and Pharisees were technically righteous. They kept all the "rules." There were rules about washing of utensils used in preparing and serving food. There were rules about holding phylacteries so as not to let them touch the dust or come in contact with ordinary people. There was a regulation about washing the hands up to the elbows on returning from market or before eating, lest inadvertent contact with Gentiles contaminate.

The strict Jews tithed even the herbs that grew around the front door of a dwelling. In short they kept the rules and supported the institution—forgetting the weightier matters of justice, compassion, and good neighborliness. They lost touch with suffering humanity.

The new order called for new righteousness. "Except your righteousness shall exceed the righteousness of the scribes and Pharisees, ye shall in no wise enter into the kingdom of heaven." The kingdom of heaven demands more than institutionalism, rule keeping, and observance of outward forms. The new righteousness begins in the heart and expresses itself in human relations. Jesus spelled out in the succeeding verses what this righteousness is. It is not really new after all. The law was given to protect the rights of others. The law worked no ill to a man's neighbor.

It is sometimes maintained that Jesus was not original, that even Maimonides had long ago stated the Golden Rule in its negative form. But what is more distinctive than the ability to take neglected truths, restate and refurbish them so that for the first time in history men everywhere begin to study them seriously? Jesus not only gave new meaning to old truths, but made it possible for man to have the power to live by these teachings. Precious little of Old Testament ethics would have ever seeped through synagogue masonry to benighted Gentiles but for the moral dynamic released by the Lord Jesus Christ producing a zealously missionary church to carry his "law" to the uttermost parts of the earth!

"Pharisees" means separatists. This exclusivism was a natural expression of a nationalistic, unspiritual conception of the law of Moses. Gentiles could enter the outer court of the Temple but could go no farther.

The scribes were the regular teachers in Israel who, having misinterpreted the law, proceeded to teach others the error. Holding tenaciously to its ritual, they missed its real significance for humanity.

The scribes and Pharisees kept the hull and threw the peanut away. The shell was everything to them. When Jesus tried to open the shell so they could see the real kernel, they

rated him a "modernist." He and the disciples were a threat
to the traditions of the fathers and must therefore be done
away with.

The Pharisees were supposed to be the best examples of
righteousness, but Christ startled his hearers with the statement that their righteousness must exceed that of the Pharisees or they could not hope to enter the kingdom of heaven.
"Exceed" here means to overflow copiously.

When tempted to question the originality of Jesus, it is
helpful to examine the carefully stated examples of the morality he demands of his disciples.

QUESTIONS FOR REVIEW AND EXAMINATION

1. What two common objects are used to symbolize the function of Christians in the world? What is meant by salt that
   has lost its savor?
2. What is Jesus' relation to the past? In what sense was the
   Old Testament law permanent?
3. What is the relationship between keeping the law and
   greatness?

FOR FURTHER STUDY

1. Compare the claims as to who the first historian was and
   formulate a definition of history on the basis of chapter 1
   of the book *The Christian Understanding of History* by
   Dr. E. C. Rust.
2. Point out the significance of history in Matthew 5:17-20
   as compared with the treatment of history given by
   Stephen, the first martyr, in Acts 7.

4

The New Morality

MATTHEW 5:21-28

THE LAW was at least 1,250 years old at the time Jesus delivered the Sermon on the Mount. But he saw more in it than any prophet or sage had ever seen. In this alone he was unique: he saw in the Law seeds of potential blessing for every man and balm for healing every ill; he applied the Law to life and human relations for the first time—and came up with something that consequently appeared new. Actually it had been there all the time, but no one would dare take it out. These principles had always existed. Things are in the Bible because they are true and are not true merely because they are in the Bible.

In six specific problems of moral conduct Jesus extends the meaning of the law: murder, adultery, divorce, oaths, retaliation, and treatment of enemies. His method is based on life; it is not the "book" approach.

I. THE PROBLEM OF MURDER (MATT. 5:21-26)

Life is man's most precious possession. As long as there is life there is hope—that there may be more than life. When life is gone, nothing else is of value in the present scheme of things. As a gift from God, life is so sacred that it must not be destroyed or marred by another. Moses decreed stern punishment for murder (Matt. 5:21); Jesus expanded the concept to include many aspects of human relationship.

43

1. The Authority of Jesus (Matt. 5:21a, 22a)

Jesus' authority supersedes that of Moses. It was "said by them of old time, Thou shalt not kill." This refers to Moses, the lawgiver twelve to fourteen centuries earlier. It was the highest revelation of moral conduct up until that time. The prophets had occasionally given glimpses of its spiritual and universal character. Now Jesus would do so fully.

"But I say unto you" has the tone of a lawgiver. It is an emphatic contrast of Jesus' interpretation of the law with the traditional view. The pronoun "I" is given extraordinary prominence in Matthew's language, showing that Jesus boldly set his authority above that of Moses.

The entire Epistle to the Hebrews magnifies the superiority of the New Covenant (Testament) to the Old, the spiritual nature of Christian salvation to Jewish legalism, and of Christ himself to Moses. "He that despised Moses' law died without mercy under two or three witnesses: of how much sorer punishment, suppose ye, shall he be thought worthy, who hath trodden under foot the Son of God, and hath counted the blood of the covenant, wherewith he was sanctified, an unholy thing, and hath done despite unto the Spirit of grace?" (Heb. 10:28–29).

The people must early recognize and respect the Christ's authority. He would appear to go further than the law, and many would question him or would accuse him of being radical or of destroying the law. Moses' rules dealt with external actions; Jesus would go on inside to the heart of man: "Do not even be angry." Thus the law is spiritual—for those who have eyes to see and a heart to love. There are more ways of killing a person than by stabbing or shooting. A successful laundry firm for years used the slogan, "Men, stop killing your wives; let us do the dirty job!"

In the march toward perfection, we must become more than mere law-abiding citizens. The Capones and Costellos make a profession of "keeping the law" while at the same time they get away with murder. Thoreau was right: "The law will never make men free; it is men who have got to make the law free. They are the lovers of law and order who observe the law when the government breaks it." Christian righteousness must exceed that of legalistic Judaism.

2. *The Inner Roots of Murder* (*Matt. 5:22*)

Murder originates in the heart. Many are the murder confessions that have ended with, "I guess I just lost my head." The word for "angry" here is the origin of our word "orgy" or fit of temper. Anger and hotheadedness may have caused as many deaths as deliberate and malicious intentions. Outward expressions of sin begin on the inside. Anger is potential criminality. Heart control begets hand control. Jesus would arrest "murder in the making" rather than wait until it is necessary to arrest a man whose foolishness has made him a murderer.

There are three phases of the inner attitude that can lead to murder: anger, scorn, and personal insult.

(1) *Anger* (*Matt. 5:22*).—Anger stimulates the nervous system by pouring powerful adrenalin into the blood stream. One speaks thoughtlessly or strikes heedlessly under this influence. Therefore Jesus stipulates the same restraint for anger that Moses does for murder: "danger of the judgment!" (Matt. 5:21-22). This refers to the court for minor demeanors in Moses' day.

In the kingdom of Christ there is no passing of judgment over which the King himself does not in some sense preside. "We must all appear before the judgment seat of Christ; that every one may receive the things done in his body, according to that he hath done, whether it be good or bad" (2 Cor. 5:10).

The expression "without cause" is not found in the very oldest copies of the Scriptures. We like this phrase because we can always find a "cause" to be angry with another when we want to! In either case it is conceivable that a man might become angry justifiably and kill in defense of loved ones. On the other hand, the scales are tilted against the tendency of either moderns or ancients who condone violence which originates in any kind of devilish temperament, from mere hotheadedness on up to "temporary insanity."

It is anger toward a "brother" (Matt. 5:22) that makes it important. All Christians are our brothers and all men are so potentially in Christ and should be treated accordingly.

(2) *Scorn* (*Matt. 5:22b*).—The attitude here is a pride perhaps akin to intellectual snobbishness resulting in calling a supposed inferior "Raca." The word in Old Testament Hebrew and Jesus' Aramaic means empty. "Raca" was probably like "empty-head," "blockhead," "stupid!" With the use of this epithet, anger has begun to vent itself in words and name calling—a sure prelude to stormy relations. Therefore the punishment is correspondingly higher, this time "in danger of the council." This is the Sanhedrin or higher court for dealing with serious offenses.

(3) *Personal insult* (*Matt. 5:22b*).—Labeling one's brother a "fool" is often enough to start a feud or a brawl. Since it is violence within an uncontrolled heart and can precipitate physical violence, it calls for the ultimate punishment of Gehenna. "Fool" in New Testament language is *mora*, from whence our word "moron." But Bible usage of "fool," especially in the Old Testament, usually points to one who is a fool morally, i.e., a wicked man. This is an attack on his character, while the former was a reflection on his mentality.

3. *The Punishment* (*Matt. 5:21–22*)

The punishment is intensified in proportion to the sin. Anger (*orga*) or a temperamental "orgy" puts one in danger of the judgment, or the lower court. This could mean death by the sword. Disrespect for another to the extent of calling him "empty-head" or "stupid" (*Raca*) was a matter for the higher council or Sanhedrin, the supreme court for the Jews. This could mean death by stoning. "*Raca* expresses contempt for a man's head—you stupid! *Mōre* [fool] expressed contempt for his heart and character—you scoundrel." [1]

Who says, "Thou fool," shall be in danger of hell fire (Matt. 5:22c). This utter irreverence for another, this debilitating disrespect for man created in God's image invokes the highest penalty: "hell fire." This means what it says. It is from the Greek Gehenna (Heb.—*gehinnom* or valley of Hinnom). A narrow valley by this name, to the southwest of Jerusalem, was a famous municipal garbage dump. It contained both wet and dry garbage. The dry, added to daily, burned incessantly. The wet, consisting of discarded meat, rags, etc., seethed with indescribable worms. Jesus said it is better to enter his kingdom one-armed or one-eyed than having two eyes and two arms "to be cast into hell fire: where their worm dieth not, and the fire is not quenched" (Mark 9:47–48).

The Lord used his figures carefully, compassionately. Scare religion? Some children have to be frightened about running out into a road of fast traffic—and then, alas, some get killed. Some adults have to smell sulphurous flames of Gehenna or come close enough to get scorched to be shocked into a realization of the heinousness of sin and the reality of its punishment.

Whatever hell (Gehenna) fire actually means, let us hold to the language of Jesus. He said, *tēn geenan tou pouros,* or the Gehenna of fire; let us not try to attenuate or improve on it. His ability as a teacher still supersedes that of others, ancient or modern.

We expect a clean housewife to have a garbage can. Dry

---

[1] Robertson, A. T., *Word Pictures in the New Testament* (Nashville: Broadman Press, 1930), I, 44.

bits of paper, dirt, strands of web and thread are useless and cast into it. As bits of bread, meat, and rags become useless, into the garbage they go. Why should not the holy God have an efficient disposal? As men persist in making themselves useless to him, they go into the garbage dump of the universe—where their worm dieth not, and the fire is not quenched! Beyond all consideration of discarding the evil and useless in the world, the moral character of God demands a hell. God would not be God if he tolerated sin, evil, rebellion, and iniquity indefinitely. This is eternal punishment, not temporary, not mere annihilation of the soul (Mark 9:47–48; Matt. 18:8; 25:41, 46; Rev. 14:9–11; 20:10, 15).

Even if a man should choose soul annihilation after a life of sin in preference to eternity in heaven with Christ following a life of Christian conduct, it would prove a baseness of character and perverted sense of values undeserving of divine mercy. It has been suggested that the hypothetical process of annihilation would be to the spirit of man in effect as awful as perpetual cremation of a live body.

In any event Jesus was not here holding out solace to the perverted and unregenerate who, in anger, scorn, and insult, fail to reverence human beings of all races. You miss many things in going to heaven, it is true, but one of them is hell. Gehenna should not be confused with Hades, the abode of departed spirits regardless of moral status.

But we should not press unduly the idea that grades of sin and correspondingly intense punishment are explicit in the teaching concerning the words "anger," "Raca," and "fool." They all add up to the fact that Christ not only forbids murder but also anger with any overt or oral expressions thereof. But does not Paul say, "Be ye angry, and sin not"? (Eph. 4:26). The "Be ye angry" is not a command but a conditional imperative: "If you become angry, be sure you do not sin." It is the tone of a parent to a child about to do a forbidden thing: "Do it, but watch out for what happens!"

4. Maintaining Right Human Relationships
(*Matt. 5:23–26*)

(1) *Necessary to worship* (*vv. 23–24*).—Good human relations are prerequisite to acceptable worship. Worship in Christ's kingdom is one of the highest functions of which man is capable. But it is not to be entered into lightly. There should be a thoughtful transition from the world to the sanctuary. As the bird dog coming from the hunt has picked up many cockleburs, so the worshiper has much that is earthy clinging to him as he starts to church. The prickly burr of broken fellowship must be sloughed off ere he enters God's house.

Suppose the man has already entered the sanctuary and the collection plates are about to be passed. At this point he remembers a brother with whom he has had an altercation. Jesus said he should at once abandon his offering there, get up, go out, and make up with his brother. "If thou bring thy gift to the altar, and there rememberest" the broken fellowship, turn around, depart from the sanctuary, and seek out the estranged brother.

This procedure cannot be used as a clever dodge of the collection plate. Jesus did not state this principle to minimize tithes and offerings. Rather does it emphasize that money coming from proud hands guided by an unreconciled heart is not acceptable. The Lord wants not your money so much as he wants you with a pure heart.

Money is not wanted if it comes from one holding a grudge, unwilling to go the second mile in order to be brotherly. Sanctified silver cannot veneer an unsanctified soul. Christ guards his altar from the breaking in of a profane or bitter spirit presuming to make up in money for what is lacking in humility and love.

Jesus exalted true giving in his commendation of the widow who gave her last mite. He excoriated those who

would give money but not love. Some would hide the Bible
with their pocketbook; others would hide their pocketbook
with the Bible. The two should be correlated.

The seriousness of right relations to others is stressed by
the warning about going to the altar to make an offering and
"there rememberest that thy brother hath aught against
thee." You should stop and set things right. "Brother" has the
broad application as in the case of "neighbour" in Luke
10:36. It is not "if thou hast aught against thy brother" but
"if he has aught against thee."

Your conscience may be clear. The misunderstanding may
stem wholly from the other party. He may or may not have
cause for the unwholesome attitude, but if he thinks he has,
it is the duty of the worshiper to go seek reconciliation. The
gift should be left before the altar until you "first be recon-
ciled to thy brother" (Matt. 5:24).

The cementing of brotherly relationships comes before
the support of the institution. But it is a case of "both and,"
not one of "either or." Having made up with the brother,
"then come and offer thy gift." Silver is sanctified when it is
brought by a hand that has not been withheld in fellowship
from any of God's creatures.

(2) *To be sought without delay* (*vv. 25-26*).—It is wise
to avoid pressing an issue. "Agree with thine adversary
quickly, whiles thou art in the way with him." Do not wait
awhile. Anger is dangerous, and the matter should be settled
at once. While reading this sentence, if you remember one
with whom you have broken fellowship, you should put the
book down, go out, and do your utmost to establish Christian
understanding. Postponement may lead to a worse situation.

The "adversary" is clearly the other party in a potential
quarrel. "Agree with" means simply to be friendly or kindly
disposed. If trouble persists, let it come from the other side,
not yours. It takes two to make a quarrel. Prove yourself to
be a son of God by being a peacemaker.

"In the way" refers to the right of the defendant to settle "out of court" while en route to the judge, according to Roman law. Courts are uncertain. Laws can be manipulated. It is less painful, less expensive, and less destructive of human relations not to go to court. If you win your rights, you may also gain several enemies in the process. If the decision is against you, then the worst described in verse 25 may happen: from the judge to the officer to prison. Once legal sentence has been meted out, it is in force "till thou hast paid the last farthing." This Roman coin was less than half a cent.

The law is exacting but, what is worse, the unbelieving world has seen a Christian at outs with a brother. It is far better to compromise where no serious principle is involved. We think we see principle when really there is deep-seated pride goading us on. "Dare any of you, having a matter against another, go to law before the unjust, and not before the saints?" (1 Cor. 6:1).

Christians ought to stay out of court whenever possible. They should try to settle their differences privately and personally and avoid bringing them before the church. Satan seldom has more cause to rejoice than when a church splits, goes to court to see who gets the property, and lets the newspapers advertise the squabble to the public. It would be better to sacrifice personal rights, leaving all in the hands of him who has said, "I will repay" (Rom. 13:19).

Catholic interpreters see in this Scripture passage (Matt. 5:25-26) a case for purgatory. If you do not make up with God (reconciliation) by keeping the rules of the Roman Church, then in purgatory you will pay "the last farthing." However, a priest tells me that at death *all* go to purgatory for a season, the duration of which can be shortened by obedience to the Church before death and by masses said for them after death. It is best to keep this passage where Jesus did—strictly in its own habitat of human relations.

II. THE PROBLEM OF ADULTERY (MATT. 5:27–30)

Again, in dealing with human lust, Jesus goes to the roots of conduct.

1. *Old Testament Teaching*

The scarlet sin was strictly forbidden in the Old Testament (v. 27). This is the Seventh Commandment (Ex. 20:14). Because of the tolerance toward polygamy, the sins of adultery and covetousness overlapped. The former was considered more an infringement on the "property" rights of another than it was an act of impurity. Out of this twilight era of moral insensitivity Jesus lifted this question into the iridescence of divine holiness. Personal purity is at stake. The question of who or what will control a man is as important here as in anger and murder.

2. *Jesus' Teaching*

Jesus' exposition of this problem was no less drastic than his approach to murder (v. 28). He speaks again in his own authority: "It was said by them of old time ... but I say unto you." And what a saying this was: "That whosoever looketh on a woman to lust after her hath committed adultery with her already in his heart."

This teaching means at least two things: First, the cause of the scarlet sin originates within the man, not outside him. He has no right to blame another. His own mind should be made up in advance concerning any such temptation. Second, if a man is emotionally untrue to his wife, he is potentially untrue to her overtly. Suppress the former and the latter is killed before it is born. "In the heart" means not only the center of blood circulation but the affections, mind, and will. This battle must be won inwardly.

This does not mean that it is just as bad to think the scarlet sin as it is to practice it. Some self-expressionists would justify animal behavior on the assumption that to suppress desire damages one's personality, that repression creates inhibitions and complexes. They overlook the glory of self-control. Actually the desires with which God endowed us at creation are sacred. They have a sublime place in the divine plan. Sin is not so much the doing of illegitimate things as it is the doing of legitimate things in an illegitimate way.

The modern extremism on this subject could destroy civilization. A drive-in theatre advertises its evening movie with the emblazoned words, "It's sexational!" For normal people sex does not have to be promoted or stimulated; for them it needs to be sublimated, restrained, and controlled until it can be expressed according to God-given time and circumstance. Movies, television, radio, and literature which remind of sex are sowing seeds of adultery in minds that otherwise might find freedom and creativity in purity. "To lust after her" means that an unholy glance can stimulate impurity. It is not the look but the lust in it that is dangerous.

The conservative Mohammedans are wrong in compelling women and girls over twelve to wear veils and cover their limbs to the ankles and elbows lest a man be tempted; they are right in assuming that man is so constituted that the less incentive or temptation, the less apt the implementing of sin. Mohammedans generally assume that if anything immoral transpires, it is the woman's fault.

"But no one ever lived up to Jesus' demand in verse 28," it is remonstrated. It is true; this is an ideal. But ideals, like untouchable beacon lights, can guide from treacherous shoals to safety. A man without high ideals is like an automobile without a steering wheel. Low thinking begets low living.

An energetic nineteen-year-old college sophomore was converted and became a preacher. Knowing the trend of the times and human weaknesses, he limited himself to one date annually until he finished graduate school—five dates in five years. He later married well; the eye and limb he had sacrificed were more than restored.

3. *Radical Measures for Curbing Lust* (*Matt. 5:29–30*)

Radical measures are necessary to keep this sin at a minimum. If the eye or hand offends, that is, causes to stumble, then amputate it. "Offend" here means ensnare or set a trap for. Christ did not call for actual mutilation of the body but rather mastery of it. The picture of plucking out an eye or lopping off a hand in order to avoid this sin intensifies the King's plea that his subjects be clean.

Whoever practices the scarlet sin cannot enter the kingdom (Gal. 5:19–21; 1 Cor. 6:9–10). Adulterers God will judge (Heb. 13:4). The greatest self-denial a man can inflict on himself here is better than suffering in hell hereafter. We have no sort of idea that the Kinsey reports included a just proportion of serious students of the Word of God.

The "eye" or "hand" in this case may refer to an individual, a social circle, a certain form of recreation, or a so-called "friend." If it is conducive to adultery, then eliminate it. Better lose a "best friend" than expose oneself to temptation. Jesus sweetly forgave the woman "taken in adultery" (John 8:4), but he strictly charged her to "go, and sin no more" (John 8:11).

4. *Punishment*

The punishment for adultery is heavy. There are no cycles of lower and higher courts to make as in the case of anger, scorn, and insult. Jesus drove straight to the ultimate: "that thy whole body should [not] be cast into hell" (vv. 28–29).

Adultery also begets much punishment ere the arrival in the place of the damned. The mental and emotional patterns are transmitted to the third and fourth generations. Unborn children will suffer because of failure to conquer this sin. Homes are wrecked. Personality is split, and the victim is crippled and inwardly disintegrated. Long after physical ineptitude has rendered literal implementation of lustful desire impossible, the patterns of base thinking leave irrepressible traces on a leering countenance.

How necessary is the goal of perfection and even then how indispensable the reservoir of forgiving grace to make real the "land of beginning again" after intermittent failures!

III. The Problem of Divorce (Matt. 5:31-32)

This discussion is practically an extension of what was said about adultery. It should be kept distinct, however, because (1) Jesus repeated his formula of authority—"by them of old time . . . but I say unto you"—and (2) because of intermittent return to promiscuity with its ill effect on home life.

1. *The Situation in Jesus' Day*

Divorce was easy in Jesus' day. If a man tired of his wife, let him give her a "writing of divorcement" and send her home. In Mohammedan countries, where four wives are permitted, the same process is still facilitated legally. But this is stated only to show the background against which Jesus spoke. We of the West have divorce statistics of our own that restrain us from casting aspersions on the system of others— one divorce for every 3.8 marriages!

2. *Jesus' Teaching*

Jesus permitted divorce for one cause: moral infidelity (fornication—Matt. 5:31). The door is left open so as not to make it necessary to live indefinitely with a moral reprobate. But this one "grounds" for divorce is specific: literal immorality. This does not include "mental cruelty," "mistreating Fifi," and other flimsy excuses for breaking up a home.

The language of the Bible is couched in terms which mean that the person must be a persistent and confirmed fornicator (protracted action). A single violation or even several should be forgiven. A woman marrying too young and later finding her husband below her cultural and mental level is not justified in (mis-) treating him in such a way that he breaks over the bounds of marital loyalty once, giving her a flimsy excuse for running to her lawyer or pastor saying, "I've got scriptural grounds for divorce now!" And what applies to the woman is valid for the man.

Many a woman has risen to heights of character comparable to perfection by putting up with the "mistake" she made at the marriage altar. She gains a crown of glory which is passed on to her children. Her patience and loyalty finally shame her husband in not a few instances into straightening up and becoming a Christian (1 Cor. 7:13–15).

More than one man has had his soul refined by living faithfully with a woman who was not what he thought she was temperamentally, socially, mentally, or even religiously. To stick it out manfully may mean steppingstones to glory. The kingdom laws of love, patience, and forbearance are needed as much here as anywhere.

3. *Divorce and Children*

The welfare of so many others is at stake. God made no provision for divorce originally; it came later because of man's "hardness of heart" (Matt. 19:8). When Jesus dealt with the divorce question, it was doubtless with children in mind (Mark 10:2–16). It is they who suffer when their parents' selfishness leads to separation.

Divorced parents sometimes are too lavish in their affection for the children. This may stem from two things: (1) a sort of subconscious compensatory gesture to numb their sense of guilt and (2) outright competition with the other parent for the child's love. Statistics verify that broken homes are the spawning ground for juvenile delinquency.

Even atheistic Russia has recently tightened divorce laws for the "good" of the nation!

Some divorced parents do well by their children. There are commendable exceptions. Some children of divorced parents do well in spite of their background. The unfortunate home life has driven them to their knees and made them cling to Christ.

4. *Some Points to Consider*

Five vital ramifications of this problem need to be faced frankly and thought through carefully. In earnestly seeking to present a united front on this widespread problem, we should none the less grant others the right to disagree. Where the Bible is explicit, the difficulty is not serious. Where it is not, we should not make the matter a basis of fellowship.

First, let us concentrate the attack, not on divorce but on the causes of divorce. Looseness between the sexes, hasty and youthful marriages, lack of advance study on areas of compatibility beginning with religion and extending through all life interests—these constitute the battleground on which to cope with the problem.

It is not uncommon for a young man without a job to marry. It is debatable whether any man should presume to marry a woman he is not yet able to support. In like manner she on her part should know something of household management and be able to produce in the kitchen something besides dainty salads and cake icings.

Second, there is the question as to whether all marriage contracts legalized by the government are also recognized in heaven. Some maintain that a "marriage" entered into while one is in an unspiritual state may turn out to be not a marriage in the eyes of God at all. After a divorce, real love followed by genuine marriage may be found, thereby relegating the first experience to the status of legalized adultery, which can be forgiven. Some marriages are made in heaven, some only in the county courthouse, it is averred.

I feel that while this philosophy seems to avoid many problems, it has the obvious weakness of opening the door to much abuse.

Third, does a divorcee ever have the right to remarry? The New Testament gives one clear justification for divorce: persistent fornication. Certainly the sinning party would seem to have no right to another marriage. Though many disagree, it would seem that the party sinned against, having justifiable grounds for dissolving the marriage, is back where he or she was at the outset and can marry again. The Bible is not explicit on this point and therefore it ought not be a matter which determines Christian fellowship.

Suppose a man was married and divorced several times before he became a Christian? Suppose he had killed two people instead of divorcing them, would divine forgiveness be equally potent in either case? What if he had lived an adulterous life without legal marriage before he does start a home recognized by both the law and the Lord?

Suppose the offending party, after the spouse sinned against has married again, now gets right with God, falls in love, and wants to marry again? We cannot afford to lose sight of God's unlimited mercy in forgiveness, nor can we become so lax in moral standards as to let anything go. A clear line ought to be drawn so that the church does not compromise with the world while extending compassion.

Fourth, should a remarried divorcee ever hold office in a church? Paul said, "Let the deacons be the husbands of one wife" (1 Tim. 3:12), and in this same chapter the moral qualifications of bishops (pastors) and deacons appear to be identical. Imagine a church officer looking out over a congregation in which there sit two or more women with whom he has lived.

Because of the influence factor, most churches refuse to have divorcees in the offices of pastor, deacon, or teacher. Such a place ought not be filled by one who, because of his or her past, would be lax or apologetic on approaching this or any other subject in the Bible. There are many other services he can render as evidence of his humility and sincerity of desire to exalt Christ Jesus.

Fifth, should the pastor perform marriage ceremonies for divorcees who have scriptural grounds for divorce? Many pastors refuse to do a ceremony for divorcees under any circumstances. Others reserve to themselves the right to say when they will and when they will not, and then do so only in those cases where their knowledge of the facts satisfies them that the grounds for divorce were scriptural. This may appear arbitrary, but the pastor has his conscience to live with.

A person desiring to remarry may distort or falsify the facts concerning the cause of the divorce. Some few pastors, because of the untruths told about the matter, have had a strictly worded vow printed, with two spaces below for witnesses, in which the divorcee desiring remarriage pledges before God and man under sacred oath that the divorce had Bible sanction. Many who said glibly that they had such sanction, on being asked to study the pledge carefully and bring it back to be signed along with two witnesses, decided they were not so sure after all if they had scriptural grounds and proceeded elsewhere for someone to perform their ceremony.

As we strive to maintain the unity of the Spirit and to help human beings who have made pitiable mistakes, let us do two things: (1) Let us make sure we try to follow the Scriptures and not permit just any kind of marriage to receive church sanction. (2) Let us be forbearing with the pastor whichever of the above policies he follows, assuming, until he proves otherwise, that he is doing his conscientious best to do what is right. Depend on it, he has enough trouble with this problem without our hatching up any for him.

Even in Nigeria, where a man with numerous wives is sometimes converted, an unwritten code makes him economically responsible for those he puts away. They are not to be mercilessly turned out, stigmatized, and possibly driven to something worse than "legalized" adultery. The Sermon on the Mount is unremitting in its demand for personal purity; it is equally insistent on mercy for the unfortunate.

QUESTIONS FOR REVIEW AND EXAMINATION

1. Name three of the six items of moral conduct in which Jesus appeared to bring a new teaching.
2. What is the meaning of "Raca" in Matthew 5:22?
3. Why are anger and lustful looks dangerous?

FOR FURTHER STUDY

1. Carefully think through and write out the difference between the moral standards as set forth in the book *The Ten Commandments* by B. H. Carroll and the moral standards of the Sermon on the Mount.
2. List the permissible cause for divorce according to the laws of your state and compare them with the cause stipulated in Matthew 5:32. Is this cause literal or figurative?

5

The New Morality—Continued

MATTHEW 5:33–48

We MOVE NOW to consider the teachings of Jesus, that for most of us, perhaps, become more frequent problems than those discussed in the last chapter.

IV. CHRIST'S TEACHING ABOUT SPEECH (MATT. 5:33–37)

The new morality in Christ's kingdom calls for simplicity and honesty of speech. It is set against the background of Leviticus 19:12, "Ye shall not swear by my name falsely." This is in effect similar to the Third Commandment, "Thou shalt not take the name of the Lord thy God in vain" (that is vainly, uselessly, or unto falsehood—Ex. 20:7).

1. *The Old Testament Law* (*Matt. 5:33*)

"Thou shalt not forswear thyself" means not to perjure thyself but rather to "perform unto the Lord thine oaths." "Perform" means pay, and thus an oath is as a debt or vow to God and must be paid.

Since oaths had become so numerous, the Hebrews evaded them by hair-splitting interpretations. The law plainly required that they should swear by the name of the true God only and not by a false one. Hence the scribes concluded that only those oaths were binding which were made in God's name, in the name of some definite aspect of his nature, or in the name of something that was obviously sacred.

The Talmud later interpreted that oaths "by heaven" or

"by earth" were not binding. The Hebrews proceeded to swear prolifically by the altar, the vessels, the lamb, by Moses and the prophets, and regarded it as insignificant. The tendency was sufficiently prevalent among early Christians that James enjoined, "But above all things, my brethren, swear not, . . . lest ye fall into condemnation" (James 5:12).

2. *Jesus' Teaching in Respect to Oaths (Matt. 5:34)*

Jesus lifted the question of honest speech out of the sea of rabbinical quibbling. The best means for avoiding false swearing is to abandon swearing altogether. Again his authority compresses a mountain of truth into a molehill of language: "But I say unto you, Swear not at all." Jesus struck deep into the heart of the matter. He would have his followers be done with external trivialities by holding to the principle of honesty involved. He thus "fulfilled" the true law again.

Does this preclude the responsibility of making oaths in court procedures? Just as divorce or killing (in self-defense) might be admissible under certain circumstances, so Jesus appears to have answered under the oath stipulated by the high priest in Matthew 26:63–64. (Compare Paul in Rom. 1:9; 2 Cor. 1:23; Gal. 1:20.) But the laws of some great nations have respected the conscience of Christians in not compelling them to swear in court. An Arab lawyer, Khalif, in Beirut, Lebanon, sometimes invoked a French law framed specifically for Baptists to excuse them from taking oath in court, and the judge acquiesced! An oath itself always implies the possibility of deceit.

Simplicity of speech is required of Christians (Matt. 5:35–37). A dishonest man might as soon lie under oath as otherwise. The great principle of reverence for truth is at stake. Why swear by the earth? It is God's footstool. Why by heaven? It is God's throne. Or by Jerusalem? It is the city of the King (Psalm 48:2).

MONTHLY REPORT OF PRESIDENT OF THE

....UNION

To Baptist Training Union
At General Monthly Officers' Council

(If you have a department director, turn this report over to him. He will report to the Training Union for all unions.)

For Month of.., 19...........

Number present in officers' council..

Did you attend monthly Training Union executive committee meeting?

....

Program committee meeting held..

Are programs planned for next month?...

Average enrolment for the past month..

Number new members during month..

When was last social held?..

Grade of union for month..

Is union Standard?.................................... . If not, name points lacking

....

....

Are officers and committees working?..

Special work done..

Plans for next month..

....

...., President

.... Union

Form BR-21—Baptist S. S. Board, Nashville, Tenn.

MONTHLY REPORT OF PRESIDENT OF THE

UNION..

To Baptist Training Union
At General Monthly Officers' Council

(If you have a department director, turn this report over to him. He will report to the Training Union for all unions.)

For Month of .... 19........

Number present in officers' council ....

Did you attend monthly Training Union executive committee meeting? ....

Program committee meeting held ....

Are programs planned for next month? ....

Average enrolment for the past month ....

Number new members during month ....

When was last social held? ....

Grade of union for month ....

Is union Standard? .... If not, name points lacking

....

....

Are officers and committees working? ....

Special work done ....

Plans for next month ....

....

.... President

.... Union

In every direction one faces the divine and sublime in life. Hebrew interpreters regarded it not as a real oath if it were in the name of heaven or of earth. Yet the swearer would hardly have used these names if he had not felt that somehow they strengthened his statement. But a man known to be honest need say no more than "Yea, yea," and "Nay, nay." More than this "cometh of evil" (or the evil one—Matt. 5:37).

Three things should incite the Christian to desist from swearing:

(1) A *mark of irreverence.*—Life is not compartmentalized into the sacred and the secular. To Jesus all of life is sacred and it should be so to us.

(2) *Useless.*—Possibly no other sin is as unnecessary as swearing. To swear by one's head can make not a hair black or white (v. 36)—nor restore it where fallen! This is not a commandment against profanity though that practice is equally unseemly in a Christian and just as useless. Profanity and swearing cling together beneath the irreverent palate. The corporate American conscience is calloused at both these points. A strike in a major plant occurred because two men were dismissed for using profanity in the presence of women workers. The strikers won out and the men were returned to their jobs! What value comes from asking God to damn anything or anybody? If it is intended as a prayer, it will hardly be heard by the holy God. If it is done lightly, then it is blatantly taking God's name in vain. Respect for womanhood, if not for God, should infuse a reverent tone in every American's language. Every woman is a mother, wife, sister, or daughter to somebody.

(3) A *mark of inferiority.*—Swearing, profanity, or plain "cussing" are not hallmarks of manhood. "Oh, hell," cries a youth—and he thinks he has said something big, when actually he has given expression to the boredom of living with an empty self. Such expressions are not the exclamations of

manhood, they are the fulminations of souls who have so
seldom been believed or heeded they think that by glossing
up a statement with such words they will get a hearing for a
change. Profanity and swearing do not prove a man's trust-
worthiness. "It is not the oath that makes us believe the man,
but the man the oath."

Some oaths and vows ought not to be kept. Better break
your word than do worse in keeping it! Jephthah vowed to
God that if he would give him the battle, he would sacrifice
the first living thing he saw on returning home. Foolish man!
On seeing his only child he cried, "Alas, my daughter! . . .
for I have opened my mouth unto Jehovah, and I cannot go
back" (Judg. 11:35 ASV). A rash oath has often been a
source of injustice to children.

An oath made in haste or ignorance contrary to the will of
God in the first place ought to be repudiated boldly and
quickly. Suppose a man or woman in a wedding agreement
has signed away the religious liberty of unborn children by
promising to rear them in a totalitarian religion that changes
and deletes the express teachings of the Word of God. He or
she ought to rescind the vow and proceed in the spirit of
Christian love and American freedom to rear the children
according to New Testament Christianity! Better still is a
teaching program in home and church that warns young people in advance of such un-American processes.

V. JESUS' TEACHING ABOUT REVENGE (MATT. 5:38–42)

In the Old Testament law limited retaliation was permitted as a restraint to violence. The Hebrews knew that
basically, "Vengeance is mine, saith the Lord." But because
of the hardness of their hearts the true law was often circum-
vented. Again we come upon one of Jesus' most difficult sayings as he shows the high cost of perfect living.

1. Old Testament Standards for Retaliation (Matt. 5:38)

The Old Testament permitted retaliation on the basis of "like for like." This was no doubt an effort to restrain men of those dark days from hotheaded and uninhibited revenge in inflicting injury far beyond what they had received. It was "an eye for an eye, and a tooth for a tooth." It has been stated lightly if tritely in the words, "Tit for tat, butter for fat; you kill my dog, I'll kill your cat." After nineteen centuries we have not progressed much farther.

Even Moses strictly condemned private and personal revenge. "Thou shalt not avenge, nor bear any grudge against the children of thy people, but thou shalt love thy neighbour as thyself: I am the Lord" (Lev. 19:18). There is always great danger to society when men take the law into their own hands, as in the pioneer days of American history. Jesus did not contradict Moses; he simply insisted on fulfilling the true purpose of the law.

2. The Pattern Given by Jesus (Matt. 5:39–41)

The authority of Christ called for a new pattern in getting along with others. His principle at first appears to be one of nonresistance. "That ye resist not evil" refers to "the evil man" who is causing the trouble, though some commentators take it to mean the devil in the man. The meaning is practically the same. The Lord illustrates with four applications of the principle.

(1) Personal affronts (v. 39).—If a man "smite thee on thy right cheek, turn to him the other also." Anabaptists of Poland and Germany long took this literally and practiced pure pacifism on the strength of it. The Quakers in many instances still do likewise. To call Jesus' command here a figure would be to avoid the issue. There was much of pacifism in our Lord, his teaching and practice. Few even

today have come as far as the deacon who prayed at the out-
break of the war: "O God, we are at war. Help us in this
fight. We know the Germans are also praying to thee for thee
to help them. What canst thou do? O Lord, at least remain
neutral." [1]

Two factors help our understanding: First, Jesus' teachings were not mere abstractions. The chief mark of wisdom is
its relevancy to life. Therefore he aimed his words directly
at specific evils and gross errors of the day. Too much violence occurred where a little giving in would have avoided
it. Jesus would have subdued the vengeful spirit of his day
by an extreme application of the principle required for
peaceful living.

Second, there was often much more to be gained by such
extreme practice than otherwise. Better permit a second
blow on the other cheek than by swapping blow for blow to
end up in a fracas that might cause you to be mauled badly
or to go beyond the vengeance permitted in the law to the
extent of rashly killing or crippling the "evil man." This is
not an altogether selfish motive. It exalts the sacredness of
personality, the dignity of man, and the value of life.

It is at least debatable whether this passage is a call for
unqualified pacifism. A man will fight if a fiend is about to
violate the honor of his home. We have police and would
hardly relish life in a wicked city without them. We have
armies as policemen on the international level, and they are
parallel to a police force.

Paul recognized the vested authority of a government;
commanded us not to resist it, to pay it tribute; called it a
guardian of the peace by "the sword" and "a minister of God
to thee for good" (Rom. 13:4). Pacifism at the personal
level; collective protection at the national level; these two

---

[1] From *The Christ of the Mount* by E. Stanley Jones. By permission
of Abingdon Press.

principles help resolve this apparent paradox for most people. If it seems that this teaching to yield makes one a virtual door mat, it should be held alongside Matthew 7 : 6!

(2) *Unseemly court cases* (*v. 40*).—This verse appears to single out lawsuits. They are to be avoided. If a man would sue for a coat, let him even have the cloak also, rather than enter a litigation that might cost more. The coat was probably an inner garment often reaching to the knees. The cloak was an outer garment worn rather loosely and perhaps usable as a covering by night.[2] To relinquish both would not leave a man naked but even if it should, the embarrassment or discomfiture would be nothing compared with the possible loss of everything to a ruthless enemy.

(3) *Public indignities* (*v. 41*).—To be imposed on or insulted publicly puts a strain on our tempers and pride. Yet a Roman soldier could legally compel a Hebrew to assist him with his burden for a mile down the road. The word "compel" comes to us through Greek and Latin from Persia and means impress or conscript temporarily for messenger work.

The soldier could compel anyone to help him with his horses and baggage up to one mile. Simon of Cyrene was compelled thus by the soldiers to carry the cross of Christ. Such "impressments" were all the more despicable and humiliating to the Jews in view of their being a conquered people of national pride and dignity.

It is not if you go one mile, but if the soldier should compel you to go one that then you should go two. He could require it legally. But deepest justice can come only from one who is willing to do more than is required. The extra you do guarantees that what is required has already been given. Law is in the first mile; love is in the second. Love includes justice, but

---

[2] Broadus, John, *An American Commentary on the New Testament,* Alvah Hovey, Editor (Philadelphia: The American Baptist Publication Society, 1886), I, 120.

justice does not necessarily include love. Justice that is not "love-lit," for example, might let a freed prisoner go out and starve to death.

There are three patterns of behavior open to us: first, unlimited revenge or animal ethics; second, limited revenge or Old Testament ethics; and third, unlimited love or Christ's ethics. Life based on law will always call for retribution; life based on love will always call for restoration.

"Second-mile Christianity" is the most refreshing quality to be seen in human character. It is going beyond duty. It is the church member who does his job well and then looks for more to do. It is the pastor who serves so faithfully as to make himself almost indispensable to his people. It is doing more than is required or expected.

The good Samaritan did his duty when he delivered the robbed and bleeding Israelite safely into the hands of the innkeeper and paid his bill. But he went beyond duty when he said, "Whatsoever thou spendest more, . . . I will repay thee." When a Christian has done his duty, he is but "half done." The spirit of "whatsoever more" works in every sphere: social, economic, domestic, and religious. A workman like this seldom has to look for a job.

(4) *Borrowing and begging* (*v. 42*).—This verse encourages generous charity. Many are in dire circumstances; emergencies can overtake any of us. Does this mean we should give to every beggar who asks for a handout?

A beloved mother always gave, often sending or taking the unfortunate into a restaurant, thereby making sure that it was food he was after. Once only she refused a beggar, at a busy intersection. He collapsed in front of a streetcar which stopped just in the nick of time. Investigation revealed that he had collapsed for lack of nourishment. The mother was ever after unrelenting in teaching her children a literal interpretation of this verse. Better give to an unworthy one occasionally than fail even once to meet the need of one truly suffering.

Lending can also be a Christian favor. The Jews were commanded not to charge one another interest (Deut. 23:19) though lending was encouraged (Deut. 15:7–11). Giving might spoil some people. Lending may be as kind an act as giving, seeing that it not only relieves an emergency but also holds the recipient to frugality, work, and a sense of responsibility.

Jesus enjoined both giving and lending in a context that suggests situations in which it would not be very pleasant. The principle at stake is that of helping one's fellow man who is truly in need, even at some sacrifice to self.

This principle is to be qualified by common sense and the teachings in other Scripture passages. God, who promises anything we ask in the name of his blessed Son, gives only when he sees fit. He will not give when we "ask amiss" (James 4:3). If a man asks for our house, car, or furniture, there may indeed be something amiss. This raises the obvious principle of giving not necessarily what he asks for, but something he needs far worse.

One of two brothers who were quarreling over their inheritance besought Jesus to make the other brother "divide the inheritance with me" (Luke 12:13). The Lord did not grant the brother this request, but he did give him a penetrating lesson on covetousness (Luke 12:15–21).

Jesus did not say, "Give to him that asketh thee everything he asks for." This would be bad for both giver and recipient. Giving money is often the easy way out. The beggar or borrower may need to hear a clear strong testimony of the power of Christ in your life. He may need just the encouraging spirit you can impart that will send him back into the raw, tooth-and-claw competition of the economic world with what it takes to conquer. He may need a copy of the

New Testament or an invitation to church along with the room or meal you provide.

An organized effort for church finance prompted a written note from a member to the pastor complaining that all he ever heard around church was giving, giving, always giving. "Thanks," wrote the pastor in reply, "for the best definition of Christianity I have ever found: giving, giving, always giving."

A woman of London's nobility was said to send often her carriage loaded with food and fruits to the homes of the unfortunate or to transport someone on an urgent trip through the rain. "No," remonstrated a commoner, "she never *sent* her carriage, she always *came* in it herself and did the job personally." What many need is *you*, a little of your time, sympathy, and understanding—the person-to-person impact of a successful Christian life upon their own.

VI. TREATMENT OF ENEMIES (MATT. 5:43–48)

We approach a climax in these teachings of Christ. We are near the summit. If we see clouds of difficulty at this point, it only means that we are nearing the top. If the previous requirements seemed lofty, these are more so. There are volumes of sermons and books on the New Testament, but fewer on the Gospels than any other part. There is still less material on Matthew 5–7, and of those few books that do deal with this section still fewer treat this passage on love of enemies.

1. *The Old Testament Teaching* (*Matt. 5:43*)

The Old Testament standard was superior to the ethics of some nations. It at least called for love of one's neighbor, which denoted serious thought on the question of human relations. As in other instances popular interpretation of

Leviticus 19:18 vitiated the true meaning and effect of the law.

Moses did command, "Thou shalt love thy neighbour," but the phrase "and hate thine enemy" was a scribal addition which the Lord sharply repudiated. The scribes and Pharisees may have sought justification from the fact that God had commanded them to treat the Canaanites severely as under Joshua they took over the land. They failed to see that this was an exception necessary to the plan of getting the Chosen People settled on a land where they could be God's agents in the historical process of revelation.

The issue revolved upon the answer to the question, "And who is my neighbour?" Moses had already expanded it to include strangers in Israel (Lev. 19:33–34). The word "neighbor" is from "nigh" "bor" meaning "nigh the border" or "dwelling nigh." But nearness itself does not necessarily insure love and peace; it sometimes means strife and tension. Those owning houses or lands next to each other may be living in hostility across from "spite fences."

The Hebrews treated members of their own tribe as neighbors regardless of how far abroad they may have been scattered; then despised the Samaritans (half-Jews) living directly between Judah and Galilee! The lawyer in Luke 10:29 made everything turn upon the question, "And who is my neighbour?" It was as though he said, "I am prepared to love my neighbor all right, but I have so much difficulty determining who he is."

Jesus exploded this faulty reasoning with the persuading account of the good Samaritan. He did not tell the lawyer the answer to his question; he asked him one instead, "Which now of these three, thinkest thou, was neighbour unto him that fell among the thieves?" The lawyer was trapped; he had to answer, "He that shewed mercy on him."

A neighbor therefore is not necessarily one who is in need

but rather one who has power to meet the need of another!
"Go, and do thou likewise" means, Be like the good Samaritan. On seeing the Jew robbed and bleeding, he did not con-
sult his commentary to see if it would permit or command
him to help this man. Instead he yielded spontaneously to a
basic law in all peoples of good will: the spirit of helpful-
ness at the sight of suffering.

All of this true neighborliness and more Jesus sees in the
old law. He must slough off from it the heathenish accretions
("and hate thine enemy") and lay bare the essence of true
love to a neighbor. This time Jesus filled the law so full it
overflowed and spilled on some of their most touchy preju-
dices. He had ceased preaching and gone to "meddling"!

2. The Christian Standard (Matt. 5:44)

The Christian ethic seeks the well-being of enemies. Jesus
asserted this on his own personal authority, "But I say unto
you, Love your enemies." There are two ways to get rid of
an enemy: kill him dead or make a friend of him. No enemy
is ever made into a friend by treating him as an enemy. This
too is a Christian distinctive, love of one's enemies. It is
hardly found in extrabiblical teachings.

How to love one's enemies is carefully spelled out in verse
44. It is no academic or passive good will. It actively seeks
the well-being of the enemy. That Jesus at some time certainly included in his teaching all these illustrations of how
to love enemies is evident from Luke 6:27–30. They point
up the contrast between love and hate, between the Christian way and the heathen way. We traverse four grades in
crossing the wide chasm between love and hate:

(1) *Love for our enemies.*—We are to love those who by
virtue of some natural circumstance of our social pattern
might be classified as enemies: the different races; capital
and labor; country yeomen and urbanites; the educated and
uneducated. "Love your enemies" is a command which shows

that Christ does not accept as "natural" any divisive factor in our social relationships. It is unnatural and the Christian is responsible for eliminating it.

(2) *Blessings for those who curse.*—We are to have kind words for those who curse us: "Bless them that curse you." To curse back could start violence. To refuse the role of enemy and assume the attitude of a friend may dissolve the evil of the imprecator. "A word fitly spoken is like apples of gold in pictures of silver" (Prov. 25:11). "A soft answer turneth away wrath: but grievous words stir up anger" (Prov. 15:1). A man being insulted was biting his lips to keep back the anger. He finally said with a well-acted laugh, "My matches are all wet; I can't get started." If he did not make a friend of the enemy immediately, he clearly won the admiration of all by-standers.

(3) *Kindness to the hateful.*—It is not enough to talk or feel love toward those who hate, it must be demonstrated in deeds. "Do good to them that hate you." A charitable deed melts much ill will. It is a pity that American feeding of Germans and Japanese since the war can be identified with a foreign policy that is designed to enhance our national security. It is equally lamentable that we have not both cultivated and claimed a definite Christian motive in foreign aid.

A more immediate application of this seemingly fantastic principle might stop much strife before it starts. This doing good to them that hate you is to be studied alongside the command to turn the other cheek (v. 39). At first blush this looks like nonresistance or passive resistance. It is resistance, but there is absolutely nothing passive about it. It is active! A man strikes you on one cheek and braces himself for the return blow. You completely take him off guard when you turn the other cheek. This he did not expect. If you do strike back, you have descended to his level, and a brawl ensues. You have let him decide the amount of strife and the kind of weapon: force.

When you turn the other cheek or give the cloak with the coat or go the second mile, you have lifted the battle from the physical realm to the spiritual. Even if you have to suffer further indignities, you do not lose in the long run. And your "love offensive" may work; it often does. The enemy tries to *misuse* you; you try to *melt* his heart. You obligate him to you by means of your goodness to him, and most human beings created in the image of God cannot escape the divine pull of such love.

Nonresistance shows weakness in you and immorality in the enemy. Passive resistance, that is, giving in grudgingly, only reveals tension from both directions. But positive and active resistance on the plane of irrepressible love and undiminishing good will delineates you as superior. You have decided what kind of battle it will be and the nature of the weapons to be used. Almighty God has decided who will be the ultimate victor on this basis.

(4) *Prayer for our enemies.*—There should be used intercessory prayer, which is the highest expression of love for those who do not only hate but would "despitefully use you, and persecute you" (5:44). To pray for such an enemy will deepen the sincerity of your concern for him. To pray for another is one of the supreme acts of love. It causes a reappraisal of the man's enmity. It sometimes results in a discovery that the cause does not altogether stem from his side. Prayer changes things—but, more important, prayer changes people. Both the pray-er and the one prayed for benefit.

Those who despitefully use and those who persecute are practically the same. The omission of the former from the oldest manuscripts is therefore not important. Whether it be one who violently persecutes or one who nags and obstructs, he needs to be treated with the Christian's sharpest weapon: prayer.

"You cannot safely practice the Sermon on the Mount on gorillas," remonstrated a friend as he tried to recoil from all responsibility for infusing new life in human relations. Two things are grossly wrong with this: first, Jesus did not guarantee the physical safety of his followers; and, second, he assumed that men are not gorillas, that the image of the divine in every man makes him susceptible to grace and mercy when extended to or demonstrated before him.

But let us face it frankly; there are some men who still behave like soulless animals. Some of us are going to get hurt, therefore, if we take Jesus seriously. He plainly warned, "If any man would come after me, let him deny himself, and take up his cross daily, and follow me" (Luke 9:23 ASV). A crossless Christianity may be more comfortable, but it is also less convincing.

The Lord showed the true nature of all these very human, down-to-earth relations set forth in this teaching up to this point. Somebody must be prepared to give in, to make a concession, yes, to give up his rights if necessary. In situations that could lead to murder, divorce, or revenge, somebody must be willing to yield a point, even forego a right in order to keep the peace. It is a pagan philosophy that calls for a duel, divorce, or lawsuit at the least violation of honor or personal rights.

Jesus was never more kingly than when he was under the fire of persecution. The soldiers sought him in the garden, and when he boldly stepped forward to place himself in their hands, they fell backward, not he (John 18:6). The arresters winced while the Arrested walked with a royal tread of confidence.

Then Pilate's soldiers "stripped him, and put on him a scarlet robe. And they platted a crown of thorns and put it upon his head, and a reed in his right hand; and they kneeled down before him, and mocked him, saying, Hail, King of the Jews! And they spat upon him, and took the reed and smote him on the head" (Matt. 27:28–30 ASV). Jesus never replied with so much as a word of complaint. Why did he not strike

back? He had a "right" to. But if he had, we would not be
studying this book about him!

Through all this persecution Jesus remained in the im-
pregnable citadel of forgiveness for those who hated him so.
They were the losers. He was dying, but his death would be
a ladder to heaven and diffuse all subsequent history with a
knowledge of himself. Even before Pilate the governor, Jesus
never lost balance. What a pity that "we are so often the
blundering representatives of a poised Saviour."

Pilate cringed and vascillated and did his best to do what
is impossible for a man to do: remain neutral when basic
moral and spiritual issues are at stake. He washed his hands
publicly while his conscience smote him privately and left
him trembling in the presence of a lowly Galilean peasant!
It was not Jesus before Pilate, but Pilate before Jesus! The
former collapsed while the latter conquered.

"I like these teachings of Jesus," stated a famous Hebrew
scholar, adding, "Such a spirit is always victorious in a per-
secuting world. But Paul—we cannot take his rigid doctrinal
requirements. The Christianity of Jesus, yes; but the Christianity of Paul, no. There is an unbridgeable chasm between
them." He would then proceed with the time-worn theory
about the difference between the ethics of Jesus and the
"doctrinaire" emphasis of Paul and the apostles.

Two compelling facts reveal the absurdity of this ruse for
dodging the claims of New Testament Christianity: One is
the book of Acts, that blue steel coupling which welds the account of the historical Jesus to the phenomenon of a band of
cowardly disciples suddenly turned conquerors. Infused on
Pentecost with a spirit of courageous witnessing, they projected the gospel, established churches, and demonstrated
the ethics of the Sermon on the Mount throughout the Roman
Empire in less than a century. The other is the fact that Jesus'
teachings exude some of the same doctrinal element objected
to in the epistles; "No man cometh unto the Father, but by

me" (John 14:6 ASV); "Even as the Son of man came ... to give his life a ransom for many" (Matt. 20:28 ASV); "Baptizing them into the name of the Father and of the Son and of the Holy Spirit" (Matt. 28:19 ASV).

Of equal significance is the prolific treatment of ethics in the Epistles. Try Paul's 1 Corinthians 13; 1 Peter 2:18–25; 1 John 4:7–21; James' entire letter; or Romans 12:1–21, especially the last paragraph, and watch the so-called chasm between Jesus and Paul disappear. As Paul exhorts the Roman Christians to "overcome evil with good," he stays up on the plateau with Christ: "But if thine enemy hunger, feed him; if he thirst, give him to drink: for in so doing thou shalt heap coals of fire on his head" (ASV)—not to hurt him but to shame him into doing what is right.

This treatment of enemies makes the words of Paul and Christ sound like a well-rehearsed duet. It is true that Christ's emphasis was different. But this had the twofold purpose of giving the Hebrews an opportunity to accept the promised kingdom and to leave a foundation of moral truth by which his church should live after his ascension. The New Testament is an orderly, logical, cohesive presentation of Christianity—ultraliberal treatment of the Scriptures to the contrary notwithstanding.

The apostles call for ethical conduct not inferior to that of the Sermon on the Mount, while this body of Jesus' teaching is not altogether free of the so-called dogmatism of the Epistles. "Many will say unto me in that day, Lord, Lord, ... then will I profess unto them, I never knew you: depart from me, ye that work iniquity" (Matt. 7:22–23 ASV). King Messiah described himself as judge deciding who will ultimately enter into the kingdom of heaven!

"Golden-rule Christianity" does not go far without the Giver of the rule! We simply cannot afford to be in the position on "that day" of having failed to accept Christ and his way concerning the treatment of enemies. To heap coals of fire on their heads is best for them here—and for us hereafter.

One pastor says that the "coals of fire" principle works eleven times out of ten! One who had gossiped about or treated maliciously another is suddenly ill and in the hospital. The sight of the one wronged coming with flowers, a kind word, or a prayer thus brings tears, humility, and almost always a response of love. It works!

3. *Reasons for Loving Enemies* (*Matt. 5:45–48*)

There are three excellent reasons for loving enemies.

(1) *A mark of sonship to the Heavenly Father* (*v. 45*).—"That ye may be the children of your Father which is in heaven" does not mean that you earn the son-status by loving your enemies. Loving them is evidence that you are a son. "That ye may be" is admittedly a purpose clause in the English translation, but it is purpose of demonstration and not purpose of realization. It is introduced by a particle meaning literally "in such manner" [*opos*] ye may be sons of your Father.

This magnanimous treatment of enemies is Godlike. Children who practice it do but "take after" their Father. "Like son, like father" is true in the spiritual family as well as in the physical. Does God not treat the wicked mercifully? "He maketh his sun to rise on the evil and on the good." God controls the sun and he does not limit its life-giving radiance to good people only. Even his enemies receive blessings.

Jesus did not say, as we do, "*It* rains." He said that the "*Father* sendeth the rain." In him "all things consist." He seeds the clouds with moisture and controls the weather. His rain, simple and too often taken for granted, he sends on both the good and bad. He could withhold rain from the wicked, but it would not be like him—and we are not like him when we withhold mercy from them!

(2) *A mark of superior righteousness* (*vv. 46–47*).—Our righteousness must "exceed" that of the scribes and Pharisees

or we can "in no wise enter into the kingdom of heaven" (Matt. 5:20 ASV). "If ye love them that love you" and only them, there is no reward. Even the publicans followed this standard of ethics.

The publicans were among the most despised people of the land. They were usually natives employed by Roman officials for collecting taxes. They collected a stipulated amount for the government and could retain what they wrenched from the populace above this. Taxgatherers, never too popular anywhere, the Jews classified with "harlots" and "sinners!"

One of the chief complaints against the Master was that he frequently associated with these "publicans and sinners." Now Jesus shows that the conduct of the Pharisees was no more godly, according to his standards, than that of the publicans. These hated people loved one another after a fashion. There is a fellowship in the underworld which often restrains the wicked from talking against their own more than church members restrain themselves from gossiping about one another! To love only your own friend or kin is usually a backhanded way of loving yourself!

Suppose "ye salute your brethren only"? Again you lose your reward. "Do not even the publicans so?" (v. 47). Easterners make much of salutations and greetings, whether public or in the home. Jews ordinarily did not greet Gentiles. Mohammedans in some areas still do not salute Christians. According to Middle Eastern decorum this is plain inhospitality if not brusque unkindness.

For a Christian to be unwilling to speak to a fellow man is at least a failure in common courtesy. The Pharisees would prolong their verbose greetings to one another in market places and around the synagogues. This rude revelation of their mutual admiration society was impressive to some; to Christ it was sure evidence of low standards which disquali-

fied them from his kingdom. Matthew was a publican, but if
he was in the congregation that heard this sermon, Jesus did
not tone down his ethics to make them more palatable to him.

It is when we love those not loved by others or not lovable
to anybody that we do the Godlike thing. It is when we speak
to those whom others ignore that we practice a righteousness
above that of the Pharisees. Neglected and aimlessly wander-
ing souls have even been won to Christ and his kingdom by a
kind word of greeting accompanied by a friendly smile. This
is righteousness that is different—that puts kindness where
it is needed and not where it is expected.

(3) *A mark of perfection* (*v. 48*).—Here is that disturbing
word again. Some extremists have misinterpreted or mis-
applied it, and the rest of us have ignored it! Still Jesus says,
"Be ye therefore perfect, as your Father which is in heaven
is perfect."

"Perfect" in the Bible has three common meanings: full-
grown in body or mind, moral completeness or maturity,
and moral perfection with particular reference to love, as
here. To love friends and not enemies is incomplete love, unlike divine love, and leaves us quite imperfect. To speak only
to friends is evidence of imperfect love and shows us up as
ethically immature.

All men are perfectionists after a fashion. We demand perfect standards where it is to our advantage. We insist on
yards of 36 inches, gallons of 4 quarts, pounds of 16 ounces,
and dollars of 100 cents, and become volatile if we discover
someone has been shortchanging us. This desire for perfection deserves expression in other areas. When Christ calls for
perfection, no matter how impossible to achieve it may seem,
we must not be content with less.

Two factors intensify this call for perfection: One is the
fact that the future tense is sometimes used in the imperative sense, "Be ye therefore perfect," which is both the force
and sense here. Also the adverb "even as" says precisely that

to which the Bible language points here: "like as, according as, in the same manner as." The emphasis is upon godly conduct in this life. This is a goal we can respect. We can afford to give our allegiance to a Leader who demands something of us.

Questions for Review and Examination

1. What do you think is the reason that the teaching of the Master gives so much attention to right speech?
2. Tell some ways in which modern society considers Jesus' teaching about retaliation to be impractical. What do you really believe about its applicability to present-day life?
3. What reasons are cited for loving one's enemies?

For Further Study

1. Consider the program of your church for ministering to human want in your community. Can you suggest ways in which there could be more of the person-to-person impact in carrying out this ministry?
2. Search in your actual experience and in your reading for specific instances of the success of "resistance on the plane of irrepressible love and good will."

6

The New Motive in Religious Deeds

MATTHEW 6:1–18

STRICT HONESTY with ourselves is more difficult than honesty with others. The subconscious has a way of deluding us into thinking we perform a given task for God while it is really done for ourselves. Or sometimes we rationalize by classifying it as a "favor for the Lord" in order to clear our consciences.

Three religious acts in particular are difficult to perform altruistically: almsgiving, prayer, and fasting.

I. IN ALMSGIVING (MATT. 6:1–4)

These verses begin with, "Take heed that ye do not your alms [righteousness] before men, to be seen of them: otherwise ye have no reward of your Father which is in heaven." "Alms" in verse 1 is righteousness or religious deeds in general, while in verse 2 it is from the Greek word *eleemosenary* to which we have given the aroma of true charity. "Take heed" means hold the mind on (a matter).

1. *Cultivating Sincerity (Matt. 6:1)*

With the positive quality of controlled selfhood in the Beatitudes Jesus contrasts here an unseemly aspect of self breaking out even in religious acts. "To be seen of men" is recorded by Matthew as *theathenai,* the very word from which we get our "theater." A religious show!

It is difficult to believe that the Pharisees literally would "sound a trumpet" just before they dropped a coin into a beggar's cup or wrote out a check for the building fund. But they evidently made such a spectacle or theatrical perform-ance of it that they often received the applause of men, while some widow giving out of her penury went unpraised.

Many tithe faithfully out of a small salary and never get credit for it publicly. Others make sizable gifts spasmod-ically, and the fact is well advertised. The names of donors to some community drives are published in the daily paper. A tight-lipped financial secretary told his pastor, without calling any names, that keeping books for the church was a strain on his faith—in man, not God!

What Christ forbids is not giving publicly but giving to be seen of men. It is the motive that matters, not the manner. A public offering, a public drive for charity or church is not condemned. It is giving for the purpose of being seen that is wrong.

The desire to appear better than we are is subtle. "Ham-bone" once said, "It's bad enough to be what you is, much less try to make out like you is sump'n what you ain't." Ego and ambition are not wrong in themselves. They are neces-sary to dynamic living. But they must be channeled and sub-limated.

The old self is a shrewd actor. Having been put away by repentance and faith, it may try to come back clad in the garbs of religion and "churchianity." It is the same it always was, except that now it is "churchly." How difficult for both pastors and laymen to avoid the spirit of "Diotrephes, who loveth to have the preeminence among them" (3 John 9 ASV).

2. *Avoiding Hypocrisy* (*Matt. 6:2 ASV*)

There were "hypocrites . . . in the synagogues." The ritual called for sounding trumpets to announce a fast. Jesus may have given a subtle touch of humor and sarcasm at this point. At any rate "hypocrite" means "actor, interpreter, one who personates another." [1] It comes from a verb meaning to answer in reply and so savors strongly of the stage. It came to mean to pretend . . . to wear a mask. It is Jesus' strongest word and he reserves it for people who pretend piety.

The hypocrite's reward is fourfold: first, praise from men, some of whom may be sincere, others of whom may be doing it just "to be seen of him"; second, a constant realization that he really deserves no praise; third, an ever-present fear that men will find him out for what he is; fourth, the unpleasant knowledge of future judgment which will reveal the true state of all men.

When these hypocrites acted their parts "that they may have glory of men" (6:2 ASV), they got precisely what they wanted—but no more! "Verily I say unto you, They have received their reward" (6:2 ASV). The expression "received reward" appears often in well-preserved ancient writing (papyri) concerning commercial transactions and means received in full. That was all. No further reward on earth or hereafter would be forthcoming for these pretenders. They may keep the scribal rules ever so meticulously, but in seeking the applause of men they lost the approval of God.

The King's principle for giving is, "When thou doest alms, let not thy left hand know what thy right hand doeth" (6:3). "Alms" in these verses is literally "righteousness." It includes various religious deeds. Almsgiving, prayer, and fasting were

---

[1] Robertson, A. T., *Word Pictures in the New Testament* (Nashville: Broadman Press, 1930), I, 50.

singled out because they are nuclear points of religious activity. In popular thinking they were the essence of religious expression, explosive points for man's innate tendency to be religious and selfish at the same time. Therefore "take heed" lest the explosion be an escape mechanism which never brings the giver in line with the goal of spiritual perfection.

The command not to let "thy left hand know what thy right hand doeth" is a call for humility, honesty, and modesty. It is a combination of hyperbole and personification: one hand should keep it secret from the other that it reaches into the pocket for a sum of money to give! When you give, do not make it known so much as to yourself. This is not a command to make all giving literally secret; rather is it a warning not to make a show of giving, to avoid pride.

This warning against show must be applied according to individual need alongside Matthew 5:16: "Let your light so shine before men, that they may see your good works, and glorify your Father which is in heaven." In one sense our good works should be, even must be, seen occasionally. But some people feel that the cost in practicing Christian graces is entirely lost if they do not get credit for it from their fellow men. The fragrance of good works is wasted on desert air if it is not wafted back to them in the aroma of commendations from others.

3. *Seeking God's Approval* (*Matt. 6:4*)

Almsgiving stood high in the scale of righteous deeds set up by the Hebrews. The divine revelation of the Old Testament sets compassionate treatment of widows and orphans as a true test of religion.

"That thine alms may be in secret" (v. 4) focuses a searchlight on our motives in giving. "In secret" is a sure test of just why we give. Jesus placed no curb on doing alms. "When thou doest thine alms" shows that he both expected and intended it. No pious opposition to the method of giving used by a given church can warrant one in not giving at all. If others give out of a wrong motive, God will judge them; he will also judge us if we refuse to give at all!

The emphasis here is that if you feel some are unduly recognized for their giving while equally or more loyal givers are not publicly commended at all, keep on giving even "in secret" if need be and see what will happen. Two things: first, God will judge the hypocrites, as already pointed out; and second, he will reward you ultimately because he sees "in secret" and knows all. The church's records may contain an occasional error or even be destroyed; but God keeps his books accurately and "debit" and "credit" never get confused. Not even a cup of cold water shall go unrewarded.

The expression "shall reward thee openly" strangely enough does not contain the word "openly" in the most ancient manuscripts. Some scholars attribute it to scribal pride which after all Jesus' scathing excoriation of giving for show now demanded a show in the final assize. "Jesus does not promise a *public* reward for private piety." [2]

It is only a hair's breadth from Christianity to Pharisaism. The issue hangs on a small pin. The slightest shift and you go from safety to disaster, from white to black, from Christianity to hypocrisy. One would think that the simple Galilean disciples were far removed from the "fanfare" religion of the Pharisees. Yet Jesus said to them, "Beware of the leaven of the Pharisees" who love the chief seats and who give to be seen of men! Jesus foresaw that the greatest threat to his kingdom down through the centuries would not be the Neros, Hitlers, and Stalins; rather would it be the repetition of the foul Pharisaism of the first century in his little churches soon to spring up everywhere.

---

[2] Robertson, A. T., *Word Pictures in the New Testament* (Nashville: Broadman Press, 1930), I, 51.

II. Right Motives in Prayer (Matt. 6:5–15)

"And when ye pray" shows that Jesus assumed men would pray. The disciples asked him to teach them to pray even "as John also taught his disciples." They had been brought up on the "memorized" prayers of ritual and ceremony, but the spontaneous, unrehearsed communion of Jesus and John with the Heavenly Father was as a breath of fresh air on the Sahara desert.

1. *Errors in Praying* (*Matt. 6:5–8*)

Again Jesus warned against being "as the hypocrites are" (v. 5). Just as they put on an act in almsgiving, they also made a pious display of prayer. They prayed. Let it be credited to them that they did not repudiate prayer and prate against God in calloused secularism. Nor did their error lie in absenting themselves from the appointed place of prayer: they prayed "in the synagogues" (v. 5). "Synagogue" means come together, and was a proper place for religious devotions.

Both private and public prayer, both individual and corporate worship are indispensable. Congregational prayer can never take the place of individual prayer; and radio and TV worship can never fully replace public worship for the able-bodied. It has been suggested that if you want to estimate the popularity of a church, look at the Sunday morning crowd; of the pastor, look at the Sunday evening crowd; of God, observe the Wednesday evening prayer meeting crowd!

The Pharisees' error was not their position or posture in prayer. They would pray "standing" (v. 5). There are four possible postures: standing (Luke 18:11, 13), kneeling (2 Chron. 6:13; Acts 7:60), prostrate on the face (Matt. 26:39), and sitting. We include the last, in spite of the fact that it is least justifiable from the Scriptures, because it is so common in modern churches. If prayer is the active surging of the soul Godward, it is possible that so passive a posture as sitting is not conducive to the spirit of true prayer. On the other hand, utmost reverence is indispensable to real prayer.

We should not presume to rush into the presence of God as we rush from the street into a movie or gymnasium. Violence is done to the spirit of prayer when praying begins without conditioning the congregation for it. Some gesture or announcement should indicate clearly in every instance that someone is about to pray. Otherwise many are still scattered in their thinking or staring into space after the praying has begun. The blunder of the Pharisees lay in two serious factors.

(1) *Ostentation* (v. 5).—They prayed to "be seen of men." They were not imploring the Lord; they were impressing men. They were not moving toward heaven; they were making a show of their piety. They chose the "corners of the streets" (v. 5)—an intersection where they could be seen from four directions! The fact that God sees "in secret" from any direction did not seem to disturb them.

Mohammedans bathe hands, face, and often feet before praying in a Mosque. Ordinarily they make short shift of the lavatory preliminaries. Let them catch the eye of some tourist following them, however, and the process of bathing becomes a fascinating ritual even to the cleansing of an erstwhile neglected beard. Their performance is no less reprehensible than the church member who "for a pretext" makes long prayers impressing men with diction, enunciation, vocabulary, geographical knowledge, and orthodox theology.

Jesus' public prayers were brief, often lasting no more than a moment. His private prayers lasted all night at times and at other times began "a great while before day."

"But thou, when thou prayest, enter into thy closet" (v. 6). "Thou" is the first word in Jesus' sentence here. Its prominent place and singular number magnify the contrast between pharisaical hypocrites and genuine disciples. Jesus seldom missed an opportunity to show that there must be a difference between his followers and others.

The "secret closet" is an aid to sincerity in prayer. The word "closet" here originally meant storehouse, private chamber, or den. Even after withdrawing from the world, there is difficulty in shutting out distractions. The calls, the memories, the urgent tasks, the noise, and clamor of competitive business or hilarious play are unremitting in their effort to break through. Therefore do not start praying until "thou hast shut thy door." With no one else around to see—there is the problem, those human eyes and the nod of approval which we crave—*then* "pray to thy Father."

A distracted woman was trying to carry on a long-distance telephone conversation while the door to the booth was wide-open. "I can't hear you," she was repeating loudly when a thoughtful bystander gently closed the door—and both continued with more success their conversations.

The world must go if we would pray. Until we tune out its din and strife, real prayer is impossible. But if one announces that at such and such a time he will be in his closet for prayer, he has advertised his praying and violated the principle of secrecy.

(2) *Vain repetition* (*vv. 7–8*).—"Use not vain repetitions as the heathen do." The heathen said the same thing over and over again. They were correct in assuming that there ought to be much praying; they were wrong in thinking that mechanical babbling of the same words was praying. Whenever the saying of a memorized prayer becomes easy enough to let your mind wander from God and what you are saying, the whole process has degenerated to merely "saying prayers." The expression "use not vain repetitions" is onomatopoetic, the pronunciation of which in Matthew's language sounds like babbling (battalogasati!).

The psalmists have left some of the loftiest examples of prayer. Their examples of communion, praise, petition in suffering, assurance, aspiration, repentance, and security (Psalms 4; 8; 22; 32; 42; 51; and 91 respectively) are incomparable. There is advantage in committing such passages to memory. Many doubt, however, the wisdom of "reciting" them as a substitute for prayer. It is one thing to use them as an aid to meditation, it is another to let them take the place of praying itself.

Even the so-called "Lord's Prayer" is an example of praying directly to God without vain repetition. The Lord "himself did not use it as a liturgy. . . . There is no evidence that Jesus meant it for liturgical use by others." [3] While we should respect the feeling of those who recite the "Lord's Prayer" in concert, it is possible that the practice points in the direction of the very thing the Lord was cautioning against.

Many of us seldom really pray. To seek God's face, to bare one's heart before him, to detach oneself from the visible world and peer after the great Unseen, to intercede for a friend or loved one—these are experiences which may be facilitated in some measure by the experience and language of others but which in their deepest meaning call for going out toward God as we draw on the resources of the Holy Spirit. And then when language and mind fail "the Spirit himself maketh intercession for us with groanings which cannot be uttered" (Rom. 8:26 ASV).

Mohammedans sometimes pray repeating the expression "God is God" several thousand times after a funeral. Buddhists have been known to put a written prayer on a wheel and count it one prayer for every revolution of the wheel. The writer counted at least fifteen repetitions of prayer beginning with "Hail Mary" and also the Pater Noster (Our Father, or the Lord's Prayer) in one brief broadcast. Only with constant gratitude to the Father who has provided by the death of his Son the blood-sprinkled way to the mercy

---

[3] Robertson, A. T., *Word Pictures in the New Testament* (Nashville: Broadman Press, 1930), I, 52.

seat can any of us avoid in some measure the natural tendency to repetitious rambling.

God does not answer because of the number of times we
"repeat" a certain prayer. The heathen "think that they shall
be heard for their much speaking. Be not ye therefore like
unto them: for your Father knoweth what things ye have
need of before ye ask him" (vv. 7–8). We go to him anyhow
and our affections are strengthened and our spiritual faculties
are trained the more we pray.

2. The Model Prayer (Matt. 6:9–13)

This is the best name for these verses. The Lord's Prayer,
properly speaking, is in John 17. It is the great high-priestly
prayer uttered just prior to the betrayal and reveals the heart
of the Saviour. The Model Prayer Jesus gave as an example
or pattern. "After this manner therefore pray ye" stresses the
way in which we should pray.

"After this manner" is literally "so"—the very word used in
John 3:16, "God so loved." We should pray "so," as Jesus
taught in the succeeding verses. The privacy, directness, and
simplicity of this prayer were revolutionary in the realm of
prayer for the Pharisees. It points the way to inner confidence
for the individual while heralding principles the serious pur-
suit of which would bring social revolution. It is a sea of
meaning compressed into a few drops of language.

(1) Approach (v. 9).—"Our Father which art in heaven,
Hallowed be thy name." It is direct and reverent. There is no
ringing of bell or use of other device for securing the Lord's
attention. He is Father. That alone settles the question of
whether he hears and answers. Does a child have to send in
his card by a valet to gain an audience with his father?
Neither must you, if you are on speaking terms with God at
all, follow a circuitous route to the throne of heaven.

The word "father" is comprehensive and majestic. God is
the great uncaused Cause. He is the Creator and Progenitor

of all. Only a literal earthly father and God in heaven should ever be addressed as father. "And call no man your father upon the earth: for one is your Father, which is in heaven" (Matt. 23:9). "As a father pitieth his children"; "O righteous Father"; "I bow my knees unto the Father"; "the Father of glory"—these are but a few examples of the wealth of meaning with which the Bible enriches the word.

"Our Father" implies not only the filial relationship of son to father but also that of brother to brother. With one swift, unassuming use of the simple pronoun "our," Christ lifted prayer out of the realm of subjective striving and gave it a social conscience. The Lord had no social gospel as such; neither did he have any kind of gospel that did not begin with human need and suffering.

There is not one personal pronoun throughout this prayer in the singular number. It is *our, us, our, we, our, us, us, our* with "thy" and "thine" referring to the Father. Try repeating this prayer substituting "my" for "our" and "I" for "we." Before passing the halfway point you know something is out of kelter. There is no room for selfishness in this prayer! It has been suggested that this is "the communism of prayer"—in the true and high sense of that word, that it requires "a strong word because it is a strong prayer." [4]

The relationship of brother to brother in the kingdom of God ought to be like home ties. A travesty on modern Christianity it is that we have permitted Communists to cause hungry millions to lift up eyes of hope toward Moscow at the sound of the word "comrade" while the churches have often let the word "brother" fall to the side like an empty snakeskin shed in the early springtime.

"In secret" we must pray, Jesus had just insisted. But the example of praying he gives compels us to take our brothers into the closet with us as a prayer burden! Christ's kingdom

---

[4] Morgan, G. Campbell, *The Gospel According to Matthew* (New York: Fleming H. Revell Co., 1929), p. 61. Used by permission.

begins with the individual, but it has the social outlook. "It is based upon strong individualism—individually, a man alone with God; socially—the world on the heart, as the prayer is offered. If we learn to pray this way, a great deal of praying will cease, and a great deal of praying will begin." [5]

"Which art in heaven." Out of the sordid and unseemly, out of the suffering and selfishness of this world, Jesus talks with him whose abode is out of this world and tells us to talk to him, too. This brings together the sublime and the simple—but were they ever separate except in sophisticated minds? "In heaven" is plural; it is "the heavens." This is true in Genesis 1:1 in the first Bible reference to heaven. The Bible envisions three heavens (2 Cor. 12:2).

"Hallowed be thy name" (v. 9). This means, "May thy name be sanctified and reverenced." To the Hebrew disciples this must have meant "Jehovah," the name of their God which distinguished him from the many so-called deities of their tribal neighbors. Reverence for his name must be commensurate with the loftiness of his character.

The ancient Hebrews had sung praise to that name (Psalm 7:17), had marvelled at its excellence in all the earth (Psalm 8:1, 9), had looked upon it as a defense (Psalm 20:1), had trusted in his name (Psalm 33:21) and called upon it (Psalm 80:18), had regarded it as glorious (Psalm 72:19), and had come to view it as an eternal memorial of his character (Psalm 135:13).

The name Jehovah (literally *Jahweh*) meant that the great "I Am" was a covenant-keeping God undertaking mighty things for those in covenant relationship with him. This name, said to be framed on human lips first by Eve (Gen. 4:1), had from Moses' time particularly (Ex. 6:2) occupied a place in Jewish theology almost beyond our comprehension. They revered the name Jehovah to the extent of refus-

---

[5] *Ibid*, p. 62.

ing to pronounce it under any circumstances. This tendency was no doubt aided and abetted by the command (Ex. 20:7) not to take it in vain.

The precise pronunciation has probably been lost forever because of this superstitious attitude of the Hebrews who pronounced it Adonai (translated "Lord") wherever it occurred.

(2) *Petition for the kingdom (Matt. 6:10)*.—The order of the requests is important. First there are those things pertaining to the bringing in of God's kingdom. Prayer is first a means of getting something for God instead of for ourselves.

"Thy kingdom come" (v. 10). Many pray this prayer glibly, not really desiring the kingdom of Christ to come. It would demand too many changes in our social, economic, moral, and—yes—religious practices.

"Kingdom" is best translated "reign" here. The Hebrews thought they wanted the reign of Messiah because they envisioned him as a political king freeing them by force or magic from the yoke of the Roman Empire. Others think of Christ's reign as primarily in a millennial period, remote or near, when his righteousness shall prevail throughout the earth. This may be true—but it does not justify any tendency to postpone the practice of the teachings of the Sermon on the Mount until that time.

The ethics of Jesus require much of us; it would be pleasant to be able to avoid our responsibility for living according to Matthew 5–7 by saying that these chapters are for another generation of another era. The "reign" of Christ in one individual heart is the kingdom of God on earth to that extent. Jesus would even add, "The kingdom of God is within you" (Luke 17:21); "it cometh not with observation" because it is spiritual and moral.

You can observe (and count) the number of people who walk down the aisles during a revival, but you do not know yet whether the kingdom of God has come to them. We must wait and see if Jesus "reigns" in their hearts. We can observe, and the government can give statistical reports on, the number of families and individuals benefiting from a slum-clearance and apartment construction project. But neither social reform nor individual church membership matter much if the "reign" of Christ over men is not established.

The kingdom and the church are not coextensive. Not everyone belonging to the church is a member of the kingdom, and conceivably not every member of the kingdom is in a visible church. We accept the kingdom of God and the kingdom of heaven as synonymous. Yet the crux of the matter in both church and kingdom is the reign of Christ. "Why call ye me Lord, Lord, and do not the things which I say?" (Luke 6:46). Between the big things we cannot do and the little things we would not do, there is the danger that we shall do nothing. This one verse of Scripture may portend more tragedies for judgment day than practically any other.

"Thy will be done in earth, as it is in heaven" (v. 10). In heaven God's will is done perfectly. No form of sin or disobedience mars the peace and glory there. No longer does sin molest nor do carnal impulses make us "the bellhops of our appetites." The blessed members of Christ's kingdom are to strive to bring as much of heaven to this earth as possible. And the opportunity to make the kingdom real on earth presents itself every time you meet another human being.

When the ordinary sense of a Scripture passage makes common sense, then we should seek no other sense. This phrase is explicit: "in earth, as it is in heaven." Those teachings earlier in the sermon about anger, the second mile, adultery, and giving to all in need make sense too—if we want a heavenly life on earth. The Sermon on the Mount does not major on teaching us how to get to heaven so much as it does on how to keep hell at a minimum on earth.

Theologians often stress two categories of God's will: the efficient and the permissive. The former includes his ultimate objectives which all the demons in hell and backsliders on earth cannot thwart. The latter takes cognizance of the wayward and wicked who within certain limits can project sin to enormous proportions. Only the reign of Christ in individual hearts can reduce the latter and bring to full realization for a given generation the ultimate purposes of the Heavenly Father for his children.

"The kingdom of heaven is at hand" proclaimed Christ at the outset of his ministry (Matt. 4:17). It is still "at hand," but its full manifestation still depends on the extent to which his disciples let him reign. The scientific discoveries of recent decades are as child's play when compared with the titanic forces to be released when men link themselves to the will of God.

(3) *Petition for personal needs* (*Matt. 6:11-13*).—There are three: daily bread, forgiveness, and deliverance from temptation.

"Give us this day our daily bread" (v. 11). Bread is typical of all food. It was indeed the staff of life in the Holy Land and is still the chief item of many an Easterner's meal. There is reason to believe that "daily" means "for the coming day." [6] In any event the word stresses continuous dependence on God for the simple necessities of life. If he sends the rain and makes the sun to shine, our bread is indeed a token of divine mercy.

Modern methods of preserving and storing food have removed men far from immediate dependence on sun and rain for copious harvests of grain. Yet the Father still sits at the helm of the universe and he could turn off our prosperity in the twinkling of an eye. More than one millionaire has become a pauper overnight.

Bread is symbolic of all that is indispensable to good living. There is the "bread of life." We are to petition the Father for

---

[6] Robertson, A. T., *Word Pictures in the New Testament* (Nashville: Broadman Press, 1930), I, 53.

spiritual as well as for material food. "Man shall not live by bread alone, but by every word that proceedeth out of the mouth of God" (Matt. 4:4). The emaciated bodies of half-starved Easterners today are pitiful—but would there be nearly so many of them if there were not so many spiritually starved Westerners who omit God's Word from their daily diet?

"And forgive us our debts, as we forgive our debtors" (v. 12). To forgive means to bear away, wipe off, dismiss. "Debt" is a good analogy of sin from several standpoints. Jesus clearly used monetary debt to illustrate sin and forgiveness in a compelling parable (Matt. 18:21-35).

To wipe off or dismiss illustrates accurately what God does when he forgives our sins. He regards the debt as paid. He no longer holds it to our account, and therefore reconciliation is possible. Sin obligates us to God morally. Apart from forgiveness, disrupted relationships could never be repaired. Yet forgiveness is not cheap and easy. "I can forgive, but I can't forget" is not a Christian slogan. You may not be able to erase it from memory's scroll, but you *can* forget it to the extent of keeping it from contributing to strife, bitterness, or jealousy.

(4) *Explanation of one petition* (*Matt. 6:16–18*).—"For if ye forgive men their trespasses, your heavenly Father will also forgive you" (v. 14) does not mean that we can earn his forgiveness simply by forgiving others. Rather does it point up the spirit of forgiveness as a necessary characteristic of the true members of his kingdom. "But if ye forgive not men their trespasses, neither will your Father forgive your trespasses" (v. 15).

The petition of forgiveness is the only one in the Model Prayer which Jesus explains! Why? Surely it was not because he thought his disciples would readily understand the remainder but lack mental capacity for comprehending this single item. Rather was it because, knowing "what was in

man," he realized that it would require great effort to overcome this weakness in sinful human nature. How readily we
accept mercy only to be loathe to demonstrate it toward a
brother whose sins against us are not nearly so gross as are
our sins against God's holiness.

The word "trespass" is literally a falling to one side, a lapse,
a deviation from what is right. "Debt" emphasizes the moral
obligation involved in all sin; "trespass" points out a more
specific instance of wrongdoing. The fact that Jesus stated
this principle of forgiveness both positively and negatively
(vv. 14–15) shows how important it is in the Lord's plan for
his people.

"And lead us not into temptation" (v. 13) shows that forgiveness of past sins is not sufficient. There must be caution
and safeguards against future sin. Ancient church fathers interpreted this petition, "Do not suffer us to be led into temptation."

"But deliver us from evil" (v. 13) is a plea to escape either
the evil one (Satan) or the force of evil so prevalent both
in the individual heart and society itself. Since the Bible
deals more with specific evil, actions, and persons, this very
likely refers to the archenemy of men. In either event deliverance is most certainly possible: "There hath no temptation taken you but such as is common to man: but God is
faithful, who will not suffer you to be tempted above that ye
are able; but will with the temptation also make a way to
escape, that ye may be able to bear it" (1 Cor. 10:13).

"For thine is the kingdom, and the power, and the glory,
for ever. Amen." (v. 13). This majestic doxology was used to
conclude the Model Prayer at a very early date. The ancient
manuscripts do not have it and it is therefore omitted from
the American Standard Version of 1901.

The kingdom does belong to the Lord; it can become ours
only through his power working in us; and only thus does he
receive the glory due him on earth among men as he does in

heaven where all creatures praise him perpetually. "Amen" means may it come to pass, or so mote it be and is never more appropriately used than in petitioning for the reign of King Jesus among men on earth.

III. RIGHT MOTIVE IN FASTING (MATT. 6:16–18)

Almsgiving is an outward act in our relationship to our fellow men; prayer is an upward relation having to do with God; both should be practiced without show. Fasting is an inward relation calling for control over self, and it also should be divorced from all show. It is an experience whereby one denies himself something in one realm—the physical—in order to achieve something in another—the spiritual. Doing without food for a while may condition the body for both spiritual concentration and contemplation.

It augments the seriousness of spiritual striving when by sheer dint or will power you say, "Be still, my body, I am going to withhold food from you while I feed my soul." It does not happen often, but it is good to make the body wait while the soul is served rather than always push the soul aside so the body can retain its priority in the cafeteria line. Some churches can hardly have a reverent invitation hymn because of people rushing to avoid the wait in the long line in the downtown cafeteria. The lost note in modern Christianity is will power and self-discipline.

1. *Advantage Depends on Motive* (*Matt. 6:16*)

The advantage of fasting is lost when the motive is wrong. "Moreover when ye fast, be not, as the hypocrites, of a sad countenance: for they disfigure their faces, that they may appear unto men to fast."

Again the Pharisees drove toward one objective: the approval of men. If men could but see the countenances saddened by a prayer-burden so heavy that it gave them a hungry look, they would be pleased. With disheveled hair and long hunger lines on their faces they became a veritable "parade of piety" as they walked down the street with their religious robes flowing in the wind. "How godly," "such devotion," "what sacrificial spirits" are some of the whispered expressions of admiration which mean more to such egoists than the joy of giving one cup of cold water to a thirsty stranger. "They have their reward"—in full, again.

It is tragic when

Our very spirituality is a bid for popular approval.

Anoint your head and wash your face, said Jesus, that you may not appear unto men to fast. It is important for religion that Jesus approved the washing of the face and the anointing of the head. The body is to be restrained, but it is not to be treated as an enemy. The Christian Church has not always taken that view. Saint Abraham, the hermit who lived for fifty years after his conversion, rigidly refused from that date to wash either his face or his feet. Saint Euphraxia joined a convent of one hundred and thirty nuns, who never washed their feet and who shuddered at the mention of a bath. "Our fathers," said the Abbott Alexander, mournfully looking back to the past, "never washed their faces, but we frequent the public baths." Saint Athanasius relates with enthusiasm how Saint Antony, the patriarch of Monachism, had never to extreme old age been guilty of washing his feet. A famous virgin named Silvia, though she was sixty years of age, and though bodily sickness was a consequence of her habits, resolutely refused, on religious principles, to wash any part of her body except her fingers.[7]

Clearly, when any Christian group shows disdain for their bodies, they do violence to the spirit of Jesus' words.

2. Reward Promised (Matt. 6:17–18)

Jesus promised a reward for sincere fasting. But sincerity is present only when one endeavors to cover up the fact that he is fasting. "Anoint thine head, and wash thy face" is a command to remove all outward signs of the act. If you are

---

[7] From *The Christ of the Mount* by E. Stanley Jones. By permission of Abingdon Press.

on a fast, keep it a secret; men do not need to know about it. "Thy Father which is in secret" knows when you fast, whether men do or not. "And thy Father, which seeth in secret, shall reward thee." The reward for fasting for the right purpose is assured. "Openly" is not found in the most ancient copies of the Bible.

Fasting carries one of the most subtle appeals to selfishness and pride though it is physically an act of self-denial. It is almost a natural self-advertiser. It has a strong appeal to the group ego: People fast and tell one another about it, and then the world gets to know it. What with advertising the permissible foods for certain days, the press and commercial institutions promote the great spirit of self-denial.

3. *Practice for Today*

Is fasting a practice for New Testament Christians? Yes, if it is on a strictly voluntary and private basis. No, if it is put on a group basis and given the status of an ordinance or sacrament!

Paul charged Timothy, a young preacher, to beware of those who would come "forbidding to marry, and commanding to abstain from meats, which God hath created to be received with thanksgiving of them which believe and know the truth" (1 Tim. 4:3). Jesus gave specific instruction "making all meats clean" (Mark 7:19 ASV), that is permitting their use for food.

Fasting in special seasons is not a New Testament teaching. If it is wrong to indulge certain things at one time, it is wrong all the time. If there is an advantage in not smoking during Lent, then what is the benefit in smoking during the remainder of the year? Are real sacrifices made by such seasonal self-denial?

The deacon who said he always gave up watermelon during Lent was not speaking disparagingly of the sincere people who observe this period on the "religious calendar"; he was simply exalting the reality embedded in Paul's language: "How turn ye back again to the weak and beggarly rudiments, whereunto ye desire to be in bondage over again? Ye observe days, and months, and seasons, and years. I am afraid of you, lest by any means I have bestowed labor upon you in vain" (Gal. 4:9–11 ASV).

"Oh, my life, thou shouldest keep perpetual Lent within the secret chamber of thy being, and everlasting Easter on thy face! The inner life must always be a denial of self, but we must come to the world with a smile and a song, and the anointed head, and the washed face. This is religion, this is life." [8] The old self is obnoxious enough in its own naked carnality; but do not give it the dignity of religious regalia.

Almsgiving, prayer, and fasting compose a trinity of wholesome spiritual exercises. They are more apt to be neglected in the reverse order. When we cease all fasting (spiritual and physical), we cease to pray. When we neglect prayer, we are less likely to give alms as we should, and then all our spiritual life has sickened in some measure. Thus fasting is not an ordinance but an opportunity for intensifying spiritual concern and striving.

QUESTIONS FOR REVIEW AND EXAMINATION

1. What motive cancels the reward for religious deeds like almsgiving, prayer, and fasting?
2. Was the Model Prayer of Matthew 6:9–13 intended to be used in liturgies?
3. What is the value of fasting?

FOR FURTHER STUDY

1. List the ways in which public prayer in your church is

---

[8] Morgan, G. Campbell, *The Gospel According to Matthew* (New York: Fleming H. Revell Co., 1929), p. 62. Used by permission.

similar or different to the teachings of Christ concerning prayer in the Sermon on the Mount (Matt. 6:5–15).

2. Recall the books that you have read on prayer and review the one that has aided you the most in learning to pray. If you recall none, you might try *Prayer* by Hallesby or the treatment of prayer in chapter 15 of *The Sermon on the Mount* by Clovis G. Chappell.

7

The Old Menace of Divided Allegiance

MATTHEW 6:19-34

THE FOLLY of trying to pursue two opposite goals is the theme of Matthew 6:19-34. Man desires material wealth and spiritual values. They are at opposite poles. Is there any way of correlating the two or must he wholly relinquish one in favor of the other? Like the man who sold all he had in order to be able to purchase the "pearl of great price" so the disciple cannot hold to any possession that hinders him from undivided loyalty to Christ.

Spiritually minded people are ever in contact with material things. Clothes, food, houses, means of transportation are but a few of the "things" necessary to daily life. It would be a relief if we could detach ourselves wholly from the material structure of civilization and avoid the moral decisions involved in trying to make a living without destroying a life.

This vanishing from reality is achieved in some brands of communism where colonies eliminate the necessity of money as a medium of exchange. There is a dairy, mechanical and electrical service, storehouses for furniture and equipment, food dispensaries, and other necessities. A colonist gets what he needs from these centers; every man and woman contributes labor of some kind, and thus life moves on without money! (The colonists frequently move on as soon as they can establish promising contacts for work elsewhere.)

Christ did not major on rules to cover specific cases but eternal kingdom principles which are valid for the variegated civilizations which have made and do make human history. The Sermon on the Mount is not like the rulebook which a coach or referee pulls out for guidance concerning a specific play; it rather creates an attitude and atmosphere in which the Christian makes individual decisions as economic problems and their consequent moral dilemmas arise. But the principles are clear and the wheels touch the water at two points: concern for superfluous wealth and life's necessities.

I. CONCERN FOR SUPERFLUOUS WEALTH (MATT. 6:19–24)

There is warning and instruction; there is command and prohibition. Jesus assumed that a Christian's heart ought to be in heaven, and that such a Christian will put his treasure where his heart is and that therefore we should have less feverish activity trying to pile up fortunes on earth and more sustained effort to enrich our account in heaven. This logic is borne out in four obvious principles.

1. *The Possessive Instinct* (*Matt. 6:19–20*)

The child early learns to grasp and hold. This may be a part of the innate desire for security. In adults its extreme form is miserliness. First, there is a prohibition, "Lay not up for yourselves treasures upon earth." Many Hebrews of Christ's day were trading people; some had an uncommon love for money (as do many Gentiles). The instinct to possess possesses men of all ages and races.

The folly of laying up treasures on earth is seen in the lack of the durability and security of wealth. "Here today, gone tomorrow" is the case history of much wealth. It takes only three generations to complete the cycle: one to amass the fortune, one to inherit it, and one to dissipate it. But it often gets away more quickly!

There are moth and rust. Oriental wealth often consisted of fine cloths and fabrics. "Lydia, a seller of purple," readily comes to mind (Acts 16:14). Such wealth was easy prey to moths. Pest control and fur storage are not unlucrative businesses in the twentieth century. "Corrupt" means to cause to vanish and is precisely what moth and rust ultimately do. A piece of radium the size of a small coin and worth $80,000 is "running down," and in less than 90 years will turn into common lead!

Even when commodities had been converted into coin there was "rust" to fear. And when this destructive process did not wreak havoc on one's holdings, they were in constant jeopardy from thieves (literally robbers). They "break through" and steal. It is really "dig through" since the houses were of clay walls and sun-dried mud bricks. Frustration is seldom more intense than in the person who has just lost his wealth or savings.

This command hardly excludes the use of a bank, the making of an investment, or the purchasing of a farm; it is hyperbolical, stating tersely and absolutely the other extreme of a principle so often violated. It is like the command, "When thou makest a dinner or a supper, call not . . . thy rich neighbours; lest they also bid thee again, and a recompence be made thee" (Luke 14:12). One man used this verse as grounds for refusing to let his brother and family eat in his house! The obvious intention is that while "entertaining" there are many unfortunates who ought to be brought in and befriended—and possibly won to Him who taught us to do so! In laying up treasure just to hoard it away, we violate the spirit of stewardship.

"Lay up for yourselves." Here is a command to save—but where and how? Christ does not condemn the desire to lay up "for yourselves" (v. 20). This "passion for possession" is not wrong in itself. In fact the natural desires given us by our Creator are never inherently wrong. It is the use, abuse, misuse of them that matters. The desire is legitimate, but the Lord of life prescribes the principles according to which we may give expression to the desire—otherwise it becomes illegitimate. This applies to the desire to have and possess. It is the motive and purpose which make the difference.

When Jesus says, "Lay not up . . ." and then quickly adds, "Lay up for yourselves treasures," we need an explanation. It is his contrast in values. There is unfathomable difference between "treasures on earth" and "treasures in heaven" (v. 20). One is earthly, the other heavenly. One is spiritual, the other physical. One thinks only of the present, the other of the remote future, as well as the present. One sees only self, the other is impossible without putting others before self.

Some recoil from the concept of "reward-morality" and "fear-behavior" in the Lord's teachings. The sin in the desire to possess was not in wanting it "for yourselves," for that the Lord approves in verse 20. "Treasure up treasures" is the literal language here (v. 20), and it is still referring to the kind of treasure set forth in verse 19. While it would be glorious if men were good just "for goodness' sake," the Sermon on the Mount abounds with the theology of reward for the obedient and fearful, catastrophic end to the disobedient.

How can the disciple lay up treasures for himself in heaven? Is earth's coinage negotiable in heaven? No, but there are letters of credit accepted by heaven's bursar which are the distilled essence of one's earthly wealth dedicated to Christ.

When a Christian gives alms not "to be seen of men" but to meet the needs of suffering men, his earthly currency is being converted into the coinage of heaven. Money given in the name of Christ for the alleviation of suffering or the moral betterment of mankind will find its way to heaven. When the Lord gives out rewards on judgment day, it will be on the basis of our having let his grace beget in us compassion and generosity toward others (Matt. 25:34–36).

Surprised at the Lord's goodness to them in that final tense hour, the righteous will cry out: "Lord, when saw we thee an hungred, and fed thee? or thirsty, and gave thee drink? When saw we thee a stranger, and took thee in? or naked, and clothed thee? Or when saw we thee sick, or in prison, and came unto thee?" (Matt. 25:37–39). Then will the King of glory, the Judge of all, the Giver of the Sermon on the Mount, answer and say unto them, "Verily I say unto you, Inasmuch as ye have done it unto one of the least of these my brethren, ye have done it unto me" (Matt. 25:40).

There will be some who did not lay up treasures for themselves in heaven. "So what! They were just not as social-minded as were the others," say some. Yes, and a very unsocial reception they get: "Depart from me, ye cursed, into everlasting fire, prepared for the devil and his angels: for I was an hungred, and ye gave me no meat: I was thirsty, and ye gave me no drink: I was a stranger, and ye took me not in: naked, and ye clothed me not: sick, and in prison, and ye visited me not. Then shall they also answer him, saying, Lord, when saw we thee an hungred, or athirst, or a stranger, or naked, or sick, or in prison, and did not minister unto thee? Then shall he answer them, saying, Verily I say unto you, Inasmuch as ye did it not to one of the least of these, ye did it not to me. And these shall go away into everlasting punishment: but the righteous into life eternal" (Matt. 25:41–46). The rich are not always godly, but the godly are always rich!

Money invested in genuine evangelism—not in mere swelling of church membership rolls—in evangelism that produces disciples, learners of the Jesus-way, that wins men to life in Christ, will also meet us again in heaven. "Make to yourselves friends by means of the mammon of unrighteousness [money, 'filthy lucre']; that, when it shall fail, they may receive you into the eternal tabernacles" (Luke 16:9 ASV). With mammon (money) we send the good news of Christ and his kingdom to the lost. These saved ones now have an eternal sense of gratitude toward those who made their conversion possible.

Should these recipients of gospel grace precede their benefactors into heaven, one day they will greet the latter in glory with a great reception of welcome. Yet some cavil at an advance program that calls for 1,750 missionaries to serve abroad! The Foreign Mission Board ought to be the last agency ever to have to limit its activity for lack of funds. But evangelism does not exempt from charity any more than charity exempts from evangelism.

"Safety deposit vault for your valuables—see room clerk" is a sign in hotel rooms warning us about where to put objects of value. "Treasure up for yourselves treasures in heaven," therefore, because a fire is coming (1 Cor. 3:13) that will consume all treasure not locked away in heaven's vault. Even thieves may steal one's reputation but not his character which prompted giving to genuine causes on earth.

2. The Captivating Power of Wealth (Matt. 6:21)

"For where your treasure is, there will your heart be also." A man stays with his treasure! The "heart" in the Scriptures is more than the seat of the affections; it is the total personality including intellect, soul, will, and feeling. The heart is the capital of the soul, the headquarters of the personality!

Man is a "unit of consciousness." His body may be one place while he consciously goes around in another place in his mind. Church members anticipating a necessary absence from Sunday services would sometimes say, "I shan't be with you in body today, but I will in spirit." They were not much less a detriment to the service than many who were present in body but absent in spirit—their minds downtown at the office arranging Monday's business schedule or out on the farm planning the rotation of planting for the spring. A man is where his heart is, and his heart is where his treasure is!

It was the man's possession of wealth in the preceding verses (19–20), but here it is wealth's possession of the man! That is why it is so vital to decide where you are going to do your banking, on earth or in heaven.

As we grow older, something gets hold of us. Few men break out of the pattern of thought, conduct, and striving in which they find themselves at forty. Whatever has gripped them until that time usually clutches them as they are lowered into the grave. If it is spiritual-life, habits of prayer, study of the Word of God, kindly service, then it becomes a stronger fixity as they grow older. If it is lust, covetousness, carnality, then it surges through a man as he approaches senility, leaving his aged eyes like broken-out windows in a deserted house.

3. The Tragedy of Bad Eyes (Matt. 6:22–23)

"The lamp of the body is the eye: if therefore thine eye be single, thy whole body shall be full of light" (v. 22 ASV). The eye is the "imperial organ of the body." Far better to lose almost any other member of the body than the eye— that is, as long as the eye is "single." This means as long as it is "simple" or does not "see double."

Astigmatism is the defect which causes the eye, instead of giving one clear image, to give two or present an object entirely out of focus. To see incorrectly can be worse than total blindness. The blind man would recognize a pool by touch of his cane before stumbling into it. The man of double vision might think the pool a broader walkway and be drowned.

"Is not blindness the worst handicap a person can have?" was the question a group of theological students put to

Helen Keller. Her simple, direct but carefully worded answer was, "No, it is far worse to have eyes and not see!" In the kingdom of spiritual ophthalmology there is a real relationship between misty optic and optimistic.

The eye is not the light; it only assimilates the light into the body. If it does so properly, then "thy whole body shall be full of light" (v. 22). The eye is to the body what the mind is to the soul. The "single eye" is one which is fastened on one object clearly perceived.

"If thine eye be evil, thy whole body shall be full of darkness" (v. 23). "Evil" here does not have only a moral meaning. It is a larger word including anything calamitous, disastrous, or wicked. The "evil" eye is one that is out of order. If it presents an incorrect picture of an object or gives a false relation between that object and other things, then "how great is that darkness!" (v. 23).

4. *The Great Impossible* (*Matt. 6:24*)

"No man can serve two masters." Money is a master. Votes are bought, men are influenced, and the foreign policy of nations is bent by money. The best test of one's religion is the sudden acquisition of wealth. This reveals character more accurately than poverty.

The other master is God. Now if the heart, which is the eye of the soul, is fixed partially on God and partially on mammon (money), the man is pulled in two different directions. Man is a threefold being (body, mind, and soul) but is so constituted as to be able to give himself over to only one object of affection and remain healthy indefinitely. If he tries to "serve two masters," he will sooner or later show partiality. This will either weaken and split him inwardly or it will get him in trouble with one of the masters. He will either love the one and hate the other or vice versa. To "serve" here means to be the slave of.

"Ye cannot serve God and mammon" (v. 24). Mammon is

a Bible word for wealth or riches. Jesus did not say, "Ye should not serve God and mammon;" he declared, "Ye cannot do it; it is a moral impossibility." A man who presumes to serve both God and mammon is deluding no one but himself. When he begins "to serve" (that is, be a slave of) money, he then and there ceases to serve God. He may think he still serves the Lord. He may even come to church—in the body—and do other "religious chores." Down in his heart he has become a servant of mammon, and God gets only what is left over.

Once again we recall that Christ did not teach that it is the possession of riches which is inconsistent with his kingdom principles but rather that it is the prostitution of wealth that is damning. Jesus praised Zaccheus who, on repenting of his covetous ways, gave half (not the whole) of his goods to the poor—but was ready to go further in order to make restitution.

A recent news release tells of $20,000,000 being willed to a foundation for furthering theological education among evangelicals. The donor "being dead yet speaketh" (Heb. 11:4) and demonstrates the immortality of influence. Failure to practice this principle, as well as failure to make out one's will according to the will of God, has dissipated much money fruitlessly. Such wealth is urgently needed by Baptist colleges which are non-tax-supported always but which always need more funds to project respectably a program of learning in a Christian atmosphere.

II. Concern for the Necessities of Life (Matt. 6:25-34)

In the mad rush for wealth most men would insist that they are just out "to make a living." It is so difficult to do this they simply must shoot high and drive hard. When this is the case, Jesus reduces the solution to simplicity itself,

"Stop being anxious! God will not let you go without life's basic necessities."

"Therefore" in verse 25 points back to the moral impossibility of serving God and mammon. Jesus proceeded to show how sufficient is the help of the Lord for those who give priority rating to his kingdom. As regards superfluous wealth he taught that we must not be covetous; concerning life's necessities he showed that we must not be anxious.

Overconcern for food, clothing, and shelter can be as devastating to the poor as covetousness is to those who would be rich. The command "be not anxious" (do not take thought) occurs three times in the passage (vv. 25, 31, and 34 ASV), while the expression "being anxious" occurs at least twice more. Jesus pointed out six excellent reasons why we should not worry about the basic needs of life.

1. *Life More Important Than Things* (*Matt. 6:25*)

"The life" itself is more important than any of these things. It is the old choice between making a life and making a living. We should not set too great store on what we shall eat, drink, and wear (v. 25) because there is one thing far more important to the true disciple. That is "the life" the Lord would have him live.

God put us here for a purpose, and he will not permit us to die of want until he has accomplished his end. Anxiety consumes; worry wears; fretting frustrates. Worry does not empty a day of its problems, only of its strength.

But Jesus' argument here is from the greater to the lesser: if God gave us life, he surely will sustain it. If he gave us bodies, he surely will not let them go naked. "Life" here is the vital "animating principle." "Meat" is literally food in general. Paul would later reason similarly, "He that spared not his own Son, but delivered him up for us all, how shall he not with him also freely give us all things?" (Rom. 8:32).

2. *Man More Important Than Plants or Animals* (*Matt. 6:26*)

In verse 26 Jesus shows the superior value of man as compared to plant and animal life. "Behold the fowls of the air: for they sow not, neither do they reap, nor gather into barns." Men have often envied the manner in which birds apparently pick up their living at leisure. They do not seem to work; there is no planting, tilling, or threshing for them. Like the Hebrews in the wilderness eating manna sent daily from above, the birds seldom store away anything very far in advance.

No hoarding, no anxiety, no covetousness in the economy of the kingdom of ornithology. Then why should there be any in the kingdom of God? If "your heavenly Father feedeth them," will he neglect men made in his own image? "Are not ye of much more value than they?" (v. 26 ASV). Jesus appealed to the relationship of father to children. If sinful men admit the desire and obligation of a father to care for his children, how much more will God carry it out! Jesus referred to God as Father seventeen times in this sermon.

Jesus saw life with man and his needs at the center. All things like birds, animals, and matter were created for man. God is doing something in the universe which bestows great dignity on man. The material structure of all things is set up with a view to working out something with man at the center. The physical scheme of things is a part of the assembly line designed to help produce perfect men.

David had marvelled at the moon 240,000 miles away as well as at the stars studding the sky like "sparks off the anvil of omnipotence." He finally exclaimed, "What is man, that thou art mindful of him? and the son of man, that thou visitest him?" (Psalm 8:4). Yet David, like Jesus, would never agree that man is the result of a fortuitous combination of protozoa and amoeba. God created man in his own image, and the chief end of man is to discover and do the will of his benign Maker. Worrying about food and clothing is a hindrance to this high calling.

3. The Uselessness of Worry (Matt. 6:27–31)

We cannot add to the length of our lives by "being anxious" or "taking thought." Our life span is in the hand of God. When he is through with us, he will take us home, and not before. Our destiny, including the time and place of our death, is contained in his will and wisdom. While we must exercise care and common sense, we have little control over the ultimate length of our lives. It was wishful thinking indeed when a friend startled us by saying, "I wish I knew the very spot in which I am going to die." And then added, "I'd make sure never to be found in it!"

"Which of you by taking thought can add one cubit unto his stature?" (literally, "unto the measure of his life," though the word may also mean height—v. 27). If merely by worrying we could either make ourselves taller (as every growing boy has wished to be) or lengthen our lives, then it might be justifiable. But modern science underscores Jesus' teaching by insisting that worry actually shortens life, causes ulcers, and makes one hard to live with! Some worrying husbands growl all over the house whether it has a den or not; some fretting wives, instead of being given a bouquet and called "Rose," are given the sobriquet "Snapdragon."

The example of lilies in verses 28–29 has several fine lessons. It is as useless to worry about clothing as it is to worry about lengthening your life. The "lilies of the field" grow, but it is "how they grow" that we are to consider. "They toil not, neither do they spin."

Some aver that it is not fair for Jesus to use inanimate objects to illustrate his point: lilies are incapable of worry. This is true, but such critics miss the whole point. If lilies grow wild without human care, it points up all the more strikingly the care of God without which there would be no lilies. If he cares for the "looks of the lilies," how much more will he care for the array of human beings.

Lilies were probably of the anemone family, which cover the hillsides of Galilee prolifically for about six weeks in the spring. Of every hue imaginable, and covering the hillsides and plains like a thick Oriental carpet, when they sway in a breeze uncertain about its direction, the effect is like a kaleidoscope. Yet "even Solomon in all his glory was not arrayed like one of these" (v. 29). Solomon's wardrobe was hardly one to be found lacking in rich-colored robes of splendor—not quite as effulgent and radiant as these anemones of the Galilean hillsides. If God clothed them in attire exceeding Solomonic glory, he will at least supply human beings the basic tunics of respectability.

At this point we must beware lest it be assumed that everyone can expect a royal wardrobe of clothes. Clothes make the man—more admissible to certain circles of society! And so for women, who for years let the designers of Paris call the signals for American styles. The Lord's reasoning here assures us not of "a la mode" finery but of the necessary clothing for ordinary life pursuits. Enough to do his will is enough.

4. Anxiety a Lack of Faith (Matt. 6:30–31)

"If God so clothe the grass of the field, which to day is, and to morrow is cast into the oven, shall he not much more clothe you, O ye of little faith?" The anemones and lilies are beautiful beyond description—for less than two months. The first sirocco wind on a warm day in May or June that crawls out of the desert like hot breath from a mystical dragon sears and scorches the flowers and grass.

Inanimate objects are of no concern to God except as they affect man. Not to believe in God's providential care, therefore, is faithlessness. Man does not believe in his own worth in the sight of God when he is overly anxious about the necessities of life. Man ought to have that much faith in himself.

It is at this point that Jesus again commanded, "Therefore take no thought, saying, What shall we eat?" (v. 31). Worry about food, drink, and clothing is in effect man's way of whining, "I don't believe God cares as much for me as he does the flowers of the field, so I'll just enjoy a soliloquy of self-pity, remembering that in spite of my soul, mind, and body I'm no better than a yellow daisy or an English sparrow!"

Contrast this with the widow overheard singing on the way to sell some embroidery of her own diligent fingers, so she could buy bread:

> If the world from you withhold of its silver and its gold,
>   And you have to get along with meager fare,
> Just remember, in His word, how he feeds the little bird;
>   Take your burden to the Lord and leave it there!
>
> C. Albert Tindley [1]

Have faith in God, said Jesus, and you will cease splitting your personality. You are drawn between two loyalties: spiritual schizophrenia. Give up one—the one which is less important in the long run—and you can enjoy the other. You cannot be happy suspended between the two.

5. *Anxiety a Mark of the Unchristian World* (*Matt. 6:32–33*)

Anxiety for material things is a mark of the unchristian world. "For after all these things do the Gentiles seek." But Christ's followers are to be different from "Gentiles." Their sojourn through this world is not merely a "progressive party" in which they proceed from one luscious course to

---

[1] Copyright Hope Publishing Company, owner.

another. It is a treasure hunt in which they seek first, last, and always the kingdom of God.

As for food and clothing, "your heavenly Father knoweth that ye have need of all these things" (v. 32). But there is something more to be had than three meals a day. "Seek ye first the kingdom of God, and his righteousness; and all these things shall be added unto you" (v. 33). The treasure hunt calls for seeking after two well-defined objectives: first, the kingdom of God and, second, his righteousness. If we make God's business our business, then he assumes responsibility for our livelihood.

To seek his righteousness is the responsibility of all who enjoy this privilege. At the moment one accepts Christ as Messiah and Saviour, God *imputes* (credits) to him the righteousness of the Lord Jesus Christ. Then as he obeys the commandments of the Lord one by one, as for example those in the Sermon on the Mount, he acquires a practical righteousness which God *imparts* to him as a result of his obedience!

"All these things" includes the necessities of life. It is surprising how little we can get along on when we have to. A family returning to America lost nine of eleven handbags, leaving them without a change of clothing save the clothes for one child. But they did well for several months and were none the worse off for it.

As to food, what is really necessary? The answer of a Chinese would differ from that of a Texan. Actually little more than bread and water is all that is absolutely necessary. Anything beyond this may be a luxury. The disciples seldom had more. Poverty and wealth are often relative. Yesterday's luxuries are today's necessities. Membership in the kingdom of God is the greatest luxury of all. Other things "shall be added" according to need if we give his righteousness a priority rating.

6. The Weight of One Day's Responsibility (Matt. 6:34)

Jesus continues: "Be not therefore anxious for the morrow" (ASV). We usually worry about the future, about things which have not happened yet and which may never happen. Actually the responsibilities of any one day are enough to occupy us fully; therefore let "the morrow . . . be anxious for itself."

This is not an injunction to quit work and "toil not" like the lilies. It is no grounds for ceasing to provide for one's children in every legitimate manner. "If any provide not for his own, and specially for those of his own house, he hath denied the faith, and is worse than an infidel" (1 Tim. 5:8).

"Go to the ant, thou sluggard" (Prov. 6:6) and learn a lesson in wise but unpretentious concern for the future. He provides for tomorrow by doing what he should today. But you cannot eliminate the legitimate concerns of tomorrow by being overly concerned today. "Sufficient unto the day is the evil thereof" (v. 34). "Evil" here is not sin but problems and adversity of which each day has enough without our trying to worry ahead for those of tomorrow.

QUESTIONS FOR REVIEW AND EXAMINATION

1. How can a disciple lay up treasures for himself in heaven?
2. What does it mean to say that where a man's treasure is, there will his heart be also?
3. If we put God's kingdom and righteousness first, what does God propose to do concerning the necessities of life?

FOR FURTHER STUDY

1. Analyze the stewardship program of your church as to whether it encourages the average Christian to realize

the ideal in Matthew 6:19–24. The analysis might include a suggestion as to how people of means can best be helped by the church in this regard and how people of limited means can be helped concerning worry and anxiety as set forth by Christ in Matthew 6:27–31.

2. Compare the teachings of Christ concerning worry with any reputable work on psychology, or contrast the contribution toward this problem by such books as *The Christian Pastor* by Dr. Wayne E. Oates with that of *The Power of Positive Thinking* by Dr. Norman Vincent Peale.

8

The New Manner of Dealing with Others

MATTHEW 7:1–12

CHAPTER 7 appears to some to be a loose combination of proverbs appended to an otherwise orderly discourse. This view fails to follow the underlying train of thought which Jesus set forth. Looking backward into the broad plateau of the fifth chapter of Matthew, we see that Jesus pursued the problem of human relations and the law. Then in the sixth chapter he entered into the ever fascinating subjects of religion (almsgiving, prayer, fasting—6:1–18) and the difference between making a living and vaulting covetousness. Leaving these, he returned in chapter 7 to the primary theme of the right spirit for achieving perfection in our relations with others. While some would limit the application of these verses to dealing with non-Christians, it is not probable that the Lord would have us project two sets of Christian graces.

I. THE CRITICAL SPIRIT CONDEMNED (MATT. 7:1–5)

"Judge not, that ye be not judged" (v. 1). The word "judge" may be translated condemn. While we accept the Bible warning that there is no salvation out of Christ, we are not to presume to say specifically who is lost and who is not. That is the prerogative of Christ only.

1. *Because We Shall Be Judged as We Judge* (*Matt. 7:1–2*)

One's judgment of others determines his own judgment. Thus we are not to judge another harshly. If we wore his shoes, they might make us unstable, too! The old motto is right, "There is so much good in the worst of us, and so much bad in the best of us, that it behooves none of us to say anything evil about the rest of us."

The hypercritical spirit is prevalent. The only way to avoid being talked about is to do nothing, say nothing, be nothing. We must do right and steel ourselves against the cool draft of unwarranted gossip. After all, "Who is he that condemneth? It is Christ that died, yea rather, that is risen again, who is even at the right hand of God, who also maketh intercession for us" (Rom. 8:34).

As a follower of Christ you may be criticized, misjudged, or even demonstrated to be as imperfect as you actually are. With genuine faith in Christ, you can ignore it all. Only God has the right to condemn you or lay anything to your charge. And he will not do it without first making available to you the mercies of the crucified, risen, interceding Christ.

To be censorious places one in jeopardy of judgment. "That ye be not judged" may refer either to intermittent judgments in this life or to the judgment over which Christ will preside on the last day. The unity of the Sermon on the Mount is seen in this further revelation that God's treatment of us is in some measure dependent on our treatment of others. The merciful are happy because they will receive mercy. If we do not forgive others, neither will the Lord forgive us. Therefore, "with what judgment ye judge, ye shall be judged: and with what measure ye mete, it shall be measured to you again" (v. 2).

This principle of judgment rightly serves as a restraint on some Christians when tempted to be harsh in their evaluation of others. The fact that God's judgment upon us could be our undoing is incentive to be as kind as orderliness and integrity will permit when we have it in our power to mete out justice and judgment to another. We may make an error in judging our fellow man; God will not. The best man is but a sinner saved by grace, and he dare not shrivel to a parsimonious trickle the mercy of his Saviour which came to him in a copious stream.

The command not to judge does not mean that we are never to form an opinion of others. Character evaluation is necessary for nominating committees and democratic elections. Otherwise church elections degenerate to the level of popularity contests. These verses do not contradict the principle that "by their fruits ye shall know them" (7:16 ASV). Jesus actually commanded the disciples to "judge righteous judgment" in John 7:24.

2. *Because Our Own Faults Make Us Unable to Judge* (*Matt. 7:3–5*)

The critic has his own faults to answer for. "Why beholdest thou the mote that is in thy brother's eye, but considerest not the beam that is in thine own eye?" (v. 3). The word "brother" here may refute the idea that these verses teach us how to treat nonbelievers only. On the other hand, Jesus was speaking to Hebrews and the word "brother" was used by them in referring to one another, as Christians later came to use it.

A "beam" is what we ordinarily conceive it to be: a huge branch or piece of timber. A "mote" is a very small twig or bit of straw such as a bird might use in building a nest. It might actually fall in an eye. At any rate the difference between the size of a mote and that of a beam was such that the force of this absurd picture was not lost on the Lord's hearers. It is possible that a soft ripple of laughter played across the audience as the people visualized a man with a two-by-four protruding from his eye endeavoring to extricate a bit of fine straw from his brother's eye.

"Considerest" means set the mind to or think on. The critic Jesus portrays has been thinking too much about others and not enough about himself. Only base thoughtlessness, to say the least, would permit him to say, "Let me pull out the mote out of thine eye . . ." while a beam is still in his own eye.

Jesus' language for the captious critic was sharp, "Thou hypocrite [actor, masked face, sham, pretending to be free of faults], first cast out the beam out of thine own eye; and then shalt thou see clearly to cast out the mote out of thy brother's eye" (v. 5). What is this beam? Quite possibly the spirit of criticism itself. He who claims the right to judge others harshly has in that very claim committed a greater sin than the one he is about to criticize.

O palpitating tongue, thou unruly member! Men tame beasts, guide great ships, and extinguish great fires, but thou continuest to lash unsuspecting backs and bruise innocent hearts! (See James 3:3–8.) The relationship between an unbridled tongue and a spirit of hypercriticism is the same as that between the hand holding a dagger and a heart devoid of love. Therefore let me judge myself rigidly but others leniently.

Even when the evidence against one appears conclusive, we may judge falsely. "Drunken Driver—or Maimed Vet?" was a recent headline. "They had arrested him for drunken driving, but he insisted he was sober. Police said his eyes were glassy, his speech thick and his walk unsure. Given the usual tests, he was asked to pick up a coin from the floor but couldn't quite make it. Asked to blow up a balloon, he failed. Unquestionably a drunk!" [1] But—in court is was proved that

---

[1] *The Miami Herald*, Miami, Florida, January 22, 1955, "Drunken Driver—or Maimed Vet?" Used by permission.

wounds during World War II had resulted in destruction of one eye now replaced by a glass one and partial paralysis of the throat causing thick speech. A total of twenty-seven other injuries had necessitated the removal of a bone from one leg so that he was unable to stoop. Half a lung had been taken out and he could hardly blow up a balloon! The jury rendered its verdict—"not guilty."

What of the practice of criticizing, passing barbed resolutions at state and Convention-wide meetings condemning other religious bodies whose doctrines are unscriptural but whose eleemosynary institutions (orphanages, hospitals, and schools) far outnumber our own? This practice does not hurt them but does lose us much good will among those we should evangelize. Baptists of the past had a reputation because of what they were for, not what they were against.

The phrase "see clearly" in verse 5 is a compounded or intensified form of "beholdest" in verse 3. The man who corrects his own faults, who casts out the beam from his own eye, may be able to render genuine help to someone afterward. He will be able to see clearly, not the mote, but how to help get it out.

Sunday school teachers, deacons, and pastors, ever living in fish bowls, are to "reprove, rebuke, exhort with all long-suffering and doctrine" (2 Tim. 4:2). Their responsibility would be unbearable but for three things: a constant determination to achieve a perfect life, the sympathy of the people, and the grace of Almighty God.

The absoluteness of the teachings concerning the mote and beam is to be held alongside the necessity of helping a fallen brother see his fault in some instances: "Brethren, if a man be overtaken in a fault, ye which are spiritual, restore [set back in joint] such an one in the spirit of meekness; considering thyself, lest thou also be tempted" (Gal. 6:1). It is easy to see faults and condemn them; it is only the spirit of the cross which can temper and cleanse us so that we may claim for Christ's kingdom those we are tempted to criticize.

Most men are sin-blind when it comes to themselves or their loved ones. When David heard that a rich man had taken his poor neighbor's one and only pet lamb with which to dine a visitor instead of slaughtering one of his many fat ones, he practically tore his shirt in fury as he said that such a man ought to become "a son of death" (2 Sam. 12:5). Then Nathan used four words, "Thou art the man," which spelled out a bloody epoch to the fallen king as he confessed concerning Bathsheba, Uriah, and a weak moment that led to a bleak year.

II. WISE DISCRIMINATION COMMANDED (MATT. 7:6)

"Give not that which is holy unto the dogs, neither cast ye your pearls before swine, lest they trample them under their feet, and turn again and rend you." At first this does not seem to bear any relation to the preceding ideal concerning criticism. Actually, it balances what had just preceded. Without making it a topic of conversation, we can evaluate men realistically. If we are not to judge others carelessly, neither are we to set sacred things carelessly before those who would be sure to defile them with their reaction.

"Dogs," hardly domesticated then as now, roamed Palestine in packs, often feeding like scavengers. India and the Middle East still present such scenes. "Howling and fighting over their horrid food, they inspire intense disgust." [2] A dead dog was the epitome of all that is contemptible (2 Sam. 16:9). "That which is holy" ought not be given to dogs. This possibly refers to carcasses of animals from the altar which were supposed to be "burned without the camp."

"Pearl" was often used by the Hebrews for a "thought."

---

[2] Broadus, John A., *An American Commentary on the New Testament*, Alvah Hovey, editor (Philadelphia: The American Baptist Publication Society, 1886), I, 157.

The Old Testament background concerning the attitude of the Chosen People toward pork made "swine" the last object to be pleasantly associated with pearls. "Dogs" and "swine" hardly represent two different classes of people but combine effectively in saying that, alas, there are those in the world who profane the gospel or kindness when offered them.

A pastor who has sometimes in mistaken zeal tried to convert a drunk man, a Christian who has exposed the intimate feelings of his heart for Christ to people who were in no wise able to apprehend, a teacher who has presented a too advanced area of truth for the moral level of a gross sinner—these are possible examples of what Jesus warns against. Turning the other cheek, giving to beggars are not to be divorced from all discretion.

Peter helps us here as one Scripture passage interprets another Scripture passage. Beginning a lengthy exposé of false teachers he concluded, "But it is happened unto them according to the true proverb, The dog is turned to his own vomit again; and the sow that was washed to her wallowing in the mire" (2 Peter 2:22). This is not "falling from grace." It is a case of prophets who were false to begin with (2 Peter 2:1) finally being exposed and put in their place. They posed as God's men and then opposed the truth. They feigned purity and then followed putrefaction.

If out of a sense of intellectual pride you call a preacher merely because he is an erudite urbanite in contrast to the rustic yeoman recently resigned, do not be surprised if the church atrophies. If out of a feeling of superficial kindliness you put a man on "the official board" solely because he has money, do not be surprised if you get something besides money. Without unfairly pressing the bestial aspect of the figure Jesus employed, the principle of not putting certain sacred things within the grasp of those who are spiritually incapable of appreciating them is valid.

But Jesus did not dwell on this at length. He left only one scant verse. And besides, there are interpreters who maintain that it means we should not give our personalities (that which is holy) over to the dogs of appetite and the swine of desire in lustful living. While not accepting this interpretation, we must not extend the more obvious application of the verse any further than did the Lord.

All the teachings of Jesus exude the demand for more enthusiasm in promoting his kingdom, not less. We find more than enough justification for reducing our efforts as it is. There may be cases when some hog or dog will rend the heart of the faithful Christian! Some of us have been invited out as well as in. But most of us are apt to have too little zeal, not too much—especially for true evangelism and for living by the principles of the Sermon on the Mount.

At the close of the service a kindly woman would give out New Testaments and tracts to apparently interested worshipers. "I don't like the way you try to win people to the faith here right after worship," objected one of the dignified members.

"You don't like the way I do it? Then how do you do it, sir?"

"Oh, I don't do it at all."

"Then I believe God prefers the way I do do it to the way you don't do it," was the reply as she quietly walked away.

III. Prayer for Facing Dilemmas (Matt. 7:7-12)

In avoiding the spirit of judging our brothers while carefully distinguishing the reprobate, we are often baffled. Precisely where is the line that divides between what Christ would have us do and that which he would not have us do? The answer seldom lies on the surface. Different people, different circumstances and environment incite us to try to be watchful as well as winsome, to be "wise as serpents, and harmless as doves." Such uncommon difficulties call for uncommon prayer. Thus at this point Jesus gave most helpful instruction on prayer followed, strangely enough, by the Golden Rule.

1. *Persistence in Prayer* (*Matt. 7:7–8*)

"Ask, and it shall be given you; seek, and ye shall find; knock, and it shall be opened unto you." Since our relationship to our fellow man is dependent on our relationship to God, prayer is the best method for determining the action best suited to situations involving judgment and discrimination. So vital are the two commands "Judge not" and "Give not that which is holy unto the dogs," however, that they must always be approached in the spirit of prayer. This, then, is a call for importunate prayer that we make no painful error in dealing with others. To be sure, what Christ taught here concerning prayer may be given a much broader application, as in the case of other teachings (Matt. 5:48; 7:12).

"Ask" is the word for simple requesting but in itself denotes dependence. Jesus did not use it in his own praying; he approached the Father as an equal. But in many things we are in the position of beggars. Especially when in dealing with others, since we do not presume to sit on the throne of judgment and yet do not cast that which is holy before dogs and swine, we must be trusting and yet not altogether unsuspicious. We need help and should "ask" the Father for it like dependent children.

"Seek" appears to show increased concern. Having acknowledged our dependence on the Father by asking, we next seek earnestly to know his will in the matter. Again we see prayer more as a means of discovering the will of God than as a means of changing his mind.

"Knock" is intensified effort blended with a sense of dependence and a true spirit of concern. It is literally "keep on knocking," and so for "ask" and "seek." In a society of complicated relationships, religious confusion, and apostasy we simply cannot know how to apply the commands "Judge not" and "Give not that which is holy unto dogs" without much asking, seeking, and knocking.

We must stay very close to God if we are to be right with our fellow men; and we must be Christian toward them if we are to remain right with God. Spirituality is the true foundation of morality in spite of the position aired in the Aberdeen University woman's lectures over the British Broadcasting Corporation on "Morals Without Religion." Such morals are like cut flowers which cannot live indefinitely after being severed from their source of origin and life.

We have had an excellent example of morals without religion since 1917. "There is no God" cried the Communists, and by every nefarious method possible they have made a religion out of irreligion, and only real religion can save incurably religious men from it!

2. *Promise of Answer to Prayer* (*Matt. 7:8*)

Knowing our disposition to doubt, the Lord added immediately, "For every one that asketh receiveth; and he that seeketh findeth; and to him that knocketh it shall be opened." Jesus offered every inducement to prayer. He who takes the time to pray earnestly will receive an answer. For some it is yes; to others, no; to some, not yet. "O Lord, we thank thee for not answering our many foolish prayers," was often the first sentence of a beloved pastor's prayer.

An answer there will be, though according to the contingencies set forth in John 15:7 and James 4:3. The prayer must be in his name (that is, for his sake or the sake of his kingdom) and it must not be for purely selfish ends. Keep on asking, seeking, knocking. God will not send a butler to the door. The Father himself will answer.

"The King has taken us into the powerhouse of all true

living; He has brought us back to the place where wheels are throbbing with infinite energy; but at the center of the wheels is not an axle, but a heart. All the infinite dynamic of righteousness is born in the compassion of the heart of God." [3]

3. Assurance of the Right Answer (Matt. 7:9-11)

"Or what man is there of you, whom if his son ask bread, will he give him a stone?" (v. 9). "Or" seems to say that if the preceding promise is not enough to induce you to pray, then look at the fatherly nature of God in answering prayer.

The questions are couched in language which expects a negative answer to the absurd idea of an earthly father giving his son a stone for bread. The round flat discs of bread in Palestine were not unlike flat stones or pieces of shale. Similarly a father would not give a serpent when his son requested a fish (v. 10), nor a scorpion instead of an egg (Luke 11:12).

The discussion then is not whether God will answer prayer but whether he will exercise good judgment in the answering. If the earthly father is not so devoid of intelligence as to make a mistake and is not so brutal as to play pranks on his son, Almighty God will do even better.

"If ye then, being evil, know how to give good gifts unto your children, how much more shall your Father which is in heaven give good things to them that ask him?" (v. 11). "Evil" includes all imperfection, frailty, and limitations as well as sin. Imperfect men may err; the Heavenly Father cannot. On the basis of the character of God does Jesus make this appeal to his disciples to pray.

It is the Holy Spirit instead of "good things" which Jesus promised in Luke 11:13. He is the best gift of all and is all inclusive of other gifts. If prayer increases his presence in

---

[3] Morgan, G. Campbell, *The Gospel According to Matthew* (New York: Fleming H. Revell Co., 1929), p. 75. Used by permission.

our hearts, dilemmas in judging and discriminating will be both few and short-lived.

As these lines are being written, a daily paper has just come with the following caption on the editorial page: "Congressmen Arrange for Closer Contact with the Power of God." The feature writer, Caleb J. King, Sr., then proceeds with a description of "a quiet room in the Capitol set aside for prayer and meditation of members of any and all faiths who feel the need of Divine guidance in the performance of their legislative duties.

"Members who make use of this facility are assured by the Scriptures that they will be heard by the Lord and that He will bless them for their obedience to His commands. . . . A changeless pledge is written into the Word that no desire is ever sent abroad by mankind for God's guidance and help to return empty-handed—if it goes out in the right spirit." [4]

After three years of effort the sponsors of "the quiet room," Rep. Brooks Hays of Arkansas (Democrat-Baptist) and Sen. A. S. Monroney of Oklahoma (Democrat-Episcopal) brought about its "establishment for use from the beginning of the 84th Congress last Wednesday." [5]

This project is not a violation of the principle of a free church in a free state but a recognition of the need of national and world leaders for divine help in "judging" and "distinguishing" while in a cold war they must deal with men of good will as well as with some who are less free of the marks of bestiality.

IV. A SUMMARY OF THE SERMON (MATT. 7:12)

"Therefore all things whatsoever ye would that men should do to you, do ye even so to them: for this is the law and the

---

[4] *The Florida Times-Union,* Jacksonville, Florida, January 15, 1955, p. 8. Used by permission.
[5] *Ibid.*

prophets." If after earnest prayer you are still in a quandary as to how to treat someone, just ask yourself the question, "Now how would I want him to treat me if I were in his place and he in mine?" This elementary process often will get the right answer more quickly than prayer!

Praying should never become a stalling process for postponing what conscience and common sense tell you to do. A lot of praying by lost men at the "altar" falls in this class. They do not have to beg God; he is ready to save the second they become willing to be saved—from their sins.

In competing for gold some denizens of our economic jungle should beware of the dictum, "Do the other fellow before he does you" and find some way to implement the Golden Rule. They that go by the sword shall perish by the sword, and they that thrive by inhuman, ruthless, monopolistic competition may not perish by it but do far worse—create a demand for revolution that will replace the system of free enterprise with pure socialism or communism.

The only thing that will save us from communism, humanly speaking, is a truly beneficent capitalism. And when we say that, we cease speaking "humanly." The Golden Rule will not work without the Giver of both the rule and the refined gold of personal righteousness imputed by faith and imparted in response to obedience to his teachings. Obviously Christ did not teach that this rule sums up all religious duties but only those to our fellow men. To love God will make us love our neighbors, but it will make us do much more.

The sages of the ages from Confucius to Hillel had stated this maxim in one form or another, though always negatively. Typical is the latter's response to a request to teach a would-be proselyte the whole law while standing on one foot: "What is hateful to thee, do not do to another." [6]

---

[6] Broadus, John A., *An American Commentary on the New Testament*, Alvah Hovey, Editor (Philadelphia: The American Baptist Publication Society, 1886), I, 161.

Jesus stated the principle positively: Don't wait until something happens, but do unto others now that which is good. Whatever Christianity is, it is not a religion of "don't's." Follow your own local church program loyally just one month and you will discover you have had no time left to get confused about any "don't's."

Jesus is truly the Giver of the Golden Rule. He stated it as a ground for positive action and living. He supplied the dynamic of personal redemption, compassion, and evangelism without which this rule would still be mummified in the aromatic spices of some Oriental mosque or European cathedral—impotent whether in its positive or negative form. But for Christ and evangelical Christianity we would not be studying it in any form.

The Golden Rule is the "law and the prophets." A resurgence of practicing it in modern church life would do more to conserve the fruits of evangelism than anything else. The Golden Rule in simple relationships makes a tremendous difference: giving the end seat of the pew to someone else; speaking cordially to others after the service is over instead of whispering to the annoyance of others during the service; remaining for the benediction instead of grasping for coat and hat and lunging (albeit on "tiptoes") for the door as soon as the invitation hymn begins; securing a substitute or notifying the proper officer instead of leaving town with a class untaught or a department piano unplayed over a week end; joining the church to visit instead of to be visited; helping to solve the church's problems instead of becoming a church problem.

This Golden Rule must be balanced with discretion. The government's representative in court need not heed the criminal who says, "Judge, remember the Golden Rule."

The father of a recalcitrant child whom he is about to cane need not be swayed by the plea, "Father, just put yourself in my place like the Lord taught in Matthew 7:12." The Word of God is infinite and accurate in application. Seeking heaven's help through prayer, the Holy Spirit, and reason, we can hope to turn the proper facet of divine wisdom upon each individual case.

Questions for Review and Examination

1. How do you explain the apparent contradiction "judge not" in Matthew 7:1 and "give not that which is holy unto dogs" in 7:6?
2. On what does God's treatment of us seem to depend in 7:7? Compare with 5:7 and 6:14.

For Further Study

Criticize your own habits in judging others in the light of Matthew 7:5. Name some specific examples that might be conceivably interpreted as casting your pearls before swine and compare them with the spirit of the Golden Rule as set forth in the book *Fifty Years with the Golden Rule* by J. C. Penney.

9

The Great Invitation

MATTHEW 7:13–27

CHRIST again called on the disciples to practice as well as hear and agree to his teachings. Having set forth in this Manifesto what membership in his kingdom involves, the Lord added in effect, "Now you see what the kingdom of heaven is like; now you understand how you must live if you become a member of it; will you enter in?"

The teachings of the sermon were rigorous, but now that the Lord came to extend an invitation he did not lessen the rigor. Rather did he again warn what a difficult life it would be. This is true evangelism. He did not "make merchandise" of the gospel, presenting it like finely polished apples covering a basket of bad ones. However, he did not let the difficulties appear as a hopeless impasse to serious men. He concluded with the parable of the house built on rock contrasted with the calamity of the one built on sand. In spite of the strict life demanded by kingdom principles, Christ urged men that they come on in and build securely on the rock.

I. THE TWO ROADS (MATT. 7:13–14)

"Enter ye in at the strait gate: for wide is the gate, and broad is the way, that leadeth to destruction, and many there be which go in thereat: because strait is the gate, and narrow is the way, which leadeth unto life, and few there be that find it."

There are two gates, two roads, two destinations. The "strait" gate is the narrow one; it is difficult to enter. There can be no excess baggage loaded to one's sides. The worldly accoutrements of covetousness, criticism, hollow religious forms, lust, spirit of revenge must all be sloughed off before entrance is possible. This is repentance—*metanoia* living.

The road itself is narrow; it requires perseverance. The destiny is life (*zoan*). "I am come that they might have *life*, and that they might have it more abundantly" (John 10:10). Everlasting (eternal) life in the Scriptures has both a qualitative and a quantitative aspect. It is of the highest quality: spiritual, satisfying, clean, invigorating. It is of infinite quantity: of unending duration. It begins on earth and is consummated in glory.

The other gate is wide, easy to enter; it opens into a road that is broad and presumably easy to travel. Its destiny is destruction and, alas, "many go in thereat." Jesus described the way of destruction first. It is a sharp warning about the simple issues involved. Evil is popular, little loneliness is experienced on the broad road. True righteousness is not the objective of "the many," and you may often have "to walk alone" but for God's presence.

Road blocks to discipleship! Look well before you start. Have you counted the cost—and compared it with the reward offered? Evangelism that does not portray this aspect of Christianity is dishonest.

A certain man would have glibly made a profession of faith or signed a church membership card by saying, "Lord, I will follow thee whithersoever thou goest. And Jesus said unto him, Foxes have holes, and birds of the air have nests; but the Son of man hath not where to lay his head. And he said unto another, Follow me. But he said, Lord, suffer me first to go and bury my father. Jesus said unto him, Let the dead [the spiritually dead] bury their dead [the physically dead]: but go thou and preach the kingdom of God. And another also said, Lord, I will follow thee; but let me first go bid them farewell, which are at home at my house. And Jesus said unto him, No man, having put his hand to the plow, and looking back, is fit for the kingdom of God" (Luke 9:57–62).

> Who answers Christ's insistent call
> Must give himself, his life, his all,
> Without one backward look.
> Who sets his hand unto the plow,
> And glances back with anxious brow,
> His calling hath mistook.
> Christ claims him wholly for his own;
> He must be Christ's and Christ's alone.
>
> JOHN OXENHAM [1]

Such invitations do not increase the "quantity" of church memberships, but they certainly improve the quality of our Christianity.

Is "life" here ultimate salvation from sin and hell to righteousness and heaven or is it the lofty life of ethical behavior and altruism prevailing throughout the Sermon on the Mount? Very probably both. The sermon majors on ethics, but when Jesus began talking about "that day" in verse 22 he made it clear that judgment in the future and ethics in the present are not unrelated.

The use of "many" (v. 13) and "few" (v. 14) implies that the great majority do not find life in Christ. At any rate the Lord seemed greatly moved that so few should respond to his call. "O Jerusalem, Jerusalem, which killest the prophets, and stonest them that are sent unto thee; how often would I have gathered thy children together, as a hen doth gather her brood under her wings, and ye would not!" (Luke 13:34). "Did Christ o'er sinners weep and shall our tears be dry? Let tears of penitential grief flow forth from every eye!"

---

[1] Used by permission of Miss Erica Oxenham, High Salvington, Worthing, England.

II. The Two Kinds of Religious Leaders (Matt. 7:15-23)

It would seem enough that it is so difficult to enter and travel the narrow way, but besides this there are those who would mislead us!

1. *False Leaders Described* (*Matt. 7:15*)

The false leaders will seem harmless enough. "Beware of false prophets, which come to you in sheep's clothing, but inwardly are ravening wolves." "False prophets" in the New Testament language is literally pseudo prophets. While Christ referred primarily to the false teachers then among the Hebrews (scribes and Pharisees), he no doubt anticipated those who would later pervert Christianity. Paul (Gal. 2:4), Peter (2 Peter 3:3), and John (1 John 2:18) would be troubled greatly by these.

"Sheep's clothing" is a figure showing that pseudo prophets will appear harmless and righteous while actually they are "ravening" (devouring and tearing) wolves—not just goats. "And no marvel; for even Satan fashioneth himself into an angel of light. It is no great thing therefore if his ministers also fashion themselves as ministers of righteousness; whose end shall be according to their works" (2 Cor. 11:14-15 ASV). Some church members never get excited over the full orbed truth of God's Word but do get taken in by some "ism" and try to move heaven and earth in promoting it.

2. *An Accurate Yardstick* (*Matt. 7:16-20*)

"Ye shall know them by their fruits." This principle is based on a simple analogy in horticulture. Grapes do not grow from thorns, nor figs from thistles (v. 16). Good trees bear good fruit, and bad trees evil fruit (v. 17). The reverse is a physical impossibility in the plant kingdom and a moral anomaly in the spiritual kingdom (v. 18).

Does the ministry produce honest, compassionate, righteous, kind people? Then trust it. Does a church or denomination pour into society a stream of benign, diligent, fair-minded, pure-minded, spiritual, humanitarian citizens? Then organize more such churches.

Does the ministry condone evil, play "footsie" with one set of dictators and oppose others later according to which is to its advantage? Does it inspire bickering, divisiveness, and strife? Then "every tree that bringeth not forth good fruit is hewn down, and cast into the fire. Wherefore by their fruits ye shall know them" (vv. 19–20).

It does not require a detective to recognize unscriptural religious leaders. "Evil fruit" is corrupt, decayed, rotten, unsound. As long as the sap of the tree is diseased, the more the tree is cultivated and pampered, the more unsound fruit there will be. "Fruit" can refer to either the kind of life or the teachings or to both, since one begets the other.

3. *The Final Judgment of Religious Sham* (*Matt. 7:21–23*)

"Not every one that saith unto me, Lord, Lord, shall enter into the kingdom of heaven; but he that doeth the will of my Father which is in heaven" (v. 21). Some praying is no more than vain repetition of the name of God. As such it is the very thing Jesus condemned in the Pharisees who made a pretense standing in the corners of the streets. By way of contrast Jesus placed the emphasis on "doing." The man who does God's will shall enter into the kingdom.

A preacher from an eastern state, with whom we certainly do not agree on many vital points of doctrine, shocked conservative Christians a few years ago with a sermon on the subject, "The Peril of Worshiping Jesus." It *is* perilous to worship him "Lord, Lord," and then deny his principles of honesty, purity, and right treatment of other races!

A cowboy put it this way: "Suppose I'm working for Rancher Jones. If I sat around just bragging on Jones to other people, a-singing pretty songs about him, that'ud be exactly what a lot of church folks are a-doin'. But that wouldn't please Jones and he'd soon hire another cow hand to take my place. But when I get in the saddle and scout over the plains and see that Jones' cattle are all right, that they get water and pasture, and keep the rustlers from stealin' em, then Jones knows that I love him and he treats me mighty good."

The peril of just worshiping Jesus! "Why call ye me, Lord, Lord, and do not the things I say"—in the Sermon on the Mount as well as in the Epistles? Failure to do the Lord's will is that which puts the ring of disaster in the word "judgment," regardless of denomination or church affiliation.

"In that day" (v. 22) refers to the final judgment and introduces one of the Lord's most difficult sayings. Many will then say, "Lord, Lord, have we not prophesied in thy name? . . . cast out devils? . . . and done many wonderful works?" "Prophesied" here means the work of a forthteller and not necessarily a foreteller. It was those who presumed to speak for the Lord, in his "name."

Regardless of their talk and works Christ will say unto them, "I never knew you: depart from me, ye that work iniquity" (v. 23). It is not, "I knew you awhile and then forgot," but rather "I *never* knew you." They were workers of iniquity or wickedness. This statement should drive every preacher and Christian to his knees to search his heart, prove his motives, and have his soul refined anew by the Holy Spirit.

Balaam for a while appeared to be a prophet with the marks of genuineness (Num. 22–24; Deut. 23:4–5; Josh. 13:22). Judas no doubt had some favorable results in his preaching and he may have worked miracles along with the other eleven for a season.

"Success" is not always a proof of divine call and approval, nor is failure evidence of the lack of it. We have entirely too many worldly criteria (size, ornamentation, statistics) by which we judge the works of men today. Good statistical reports are not wrong in themselves. We have far to go numerically before reaching the Lord's goal: "Make disciples of all nations." But to do this we must keep the expression of Christian righteousness abreast with the expansion of membership rolls. We must be moved with compassion for people, not with desire to excel in reports.

Of the five most startling facts concerning life, salvation, and eternity, at least four are explicit in these verses: (1) Not all men will be saved (v. 23)—Jesus was no universalist! (2) Apparently more responsible people ("many" in v. 13) will fail to find life in Christ than those who do ("few" in v. 14). (3) "Many" expecting to be saved will find themselves eternally lost on judgment day (v. 22). (4) There is no second chance for salvation after death and judgment (vv. 23, 27). (5) It logically follows that death-bed repentance is a frail if not futile reed to lean on, which points up the wisdom of living out the teachings of Christ faithfully from the first hearing.

III. THE TWO HOUSES (MATT. 7:24–27)

The teaching which men call the "Sermon on the Mount" is ended. Only a "closing illustration" remains and it is an earnest call for an act of faith and commitment. There is destiny in the decision. And this decision will determine the direction of all future decisions. It is doing, not hearing only, that makes the difference.

The utter simplicity, truth, and beauty of these two stories we mar by excessive explanation. There are simply two men, a wise and a foolish one. There are two houses being built, one that stands and one that collapses. There are two foundations, one of rock (obedience) and one of sand (hearing without doing). There is a testing time for each: rains, floods, winds which beat upon the houses; final judgment and all the trials and testings that may precede it in the lives of men.

There are two distinctly different climaxes: the one house stood firmly on the rock throughout the storm; the other collapsed.

Now read slowly the accounts of the two houses, noting particularly the perfect parallelism between them. Exactly alike in every detail save two: the foundation and the end. That built on the rock of obedience was safe forever. Eternal security! The one built on sand went down in calamity. Jesus did not gloss over the tragic aspect. The last six words in this sermon are, "and great was the fall thereof" (v. 27).

Jesus did not end on a "sweet note" but with a solemn warning not only to hear "these words of mine" but also to do them. This refers primarily to the words of the Sermon on the Mount but also to all the Lord's teachings. At this point we need the words of Mary spoken to the servants at the wedding feast, "Whatsoever he saith unto you, do it" (John 2:5 ASV).

The first responsibility of a Christian is to live a good life. The chief task of any preacher or teacher is to grow a majestic soul. People will not long remember what you say, but they will not soon forget you—the impact of your life upon theirs, whether it was in the spirit of self or the Spirit of Christ.

"To make men whole" the Sermon on the Mount seems to claim for its theme. An imbalance in doctrinal emphasis produces grotesque forms in Christian living.

Identifying the greatest commandment of all, Jesus did not say, "Thou shalt love the Lord thy God with all thy heart only" as though Christianity were only *adoration* of the Lord to be experienced emotionally. Nor did he say, "Thou shalt love the Lord thy God with all thine mind only" as though Christianity were mental *contemplation* alone; nor that it is, "Thou shalt love the Lord thy God with all thy strength solely" as though faith were exclusively *activation*. Still less did he say, "Thou shalt love the Lord thy God with all thy soul alone" as though Christianity were primarily a *spirit-ualization* of all of life.

Rather the command is: "Thou shalt love the Lord thy God with all thy heart, and with all thy soul, and with all thy mind, and with all thy strength" (Mark 12:30). Do we have the courage to launch out into a life of such completeness with the goal of the development of the total personality under the leadership of Jesus Christ? Dare we remain in a state of indecision in the face of "the great invitation" of Christ?

Martin Baal, in the sixteenth century, concluded after assiduous research and agonizing prayer that justification is by faith. He folded the paper on which his conclusions were written and hid them behind the stones in the wall of his monastery room. Martin Luther reached the same conclusions but had the courage to tack his ninety-five theses on the door of the cathedral. Two Martins, but history reserves its volumes only for the one who was a doer of God's will as he understood it.

Questions for Review and Examination

1. By what rule can we distinguish between true and false religious leaders?
2. In what way are the two roads of Matthew 7:13–14 alike and in what way are they unlike?
3. Explain the fact that the Sermon on the Mount begins in the Beatitudes with what disciples must *be* and then ends with emphasis upon *doing* (7:24).

For Further Study

Analyze the relationship between the invitation in 7:13 and the parable of the two houses according to the exposition of Broadus in *An American Commentary on the New Testament*.

DIRECTIONS FOR THE TEACHING AND STUDY
OF THIS BOOK FOR CREDIT

I. DIRECTIONS FOR THE TEACHER

1. Ten class periods of forty-five minutes each, or the equivalent, are required for the completion of a book for credit.

2. The teacher should request an award on the book taught.

3. The teacher shall give a written examination covering the subject matter in the textbook. The examination may take the form of assigned work to be done between the class sessions, in the class sessions, or as a final examination.

Exception: All who attend all of the class sessions; who read the book through by the close of the course; and who, in the judgment of the teacher, do the classwork satisfactorily may be exempted from taking the examination.

4. Either Sunday school or Training Union credit (*to Young People and Adults only in Training Union*) may be had for the study of this book. Application for Sunday school awards should be sent to the state Sunday school department, for Training Union awards to the state Training Union department, where forms may be secured on which to make application. These forms should be made in triplicate. Keep the last copy for the church file, and send the other two copies.

II. DIRECTIONS FOR THE STUDENT°

1. *In Classwork*

(1) The student must attend at least six of the ten forty-five minute class periods to be entitled to take the class examination.

(2) The student must certify that the textbook has been read. (In rare cases where students may find it impracticable to read the book before the completion of the classwork, the teacher may accept a promise to read the book carefully within the next two weeks. This applies only to students who do the written work.)

(3) The student must take a written examination, making a minimum grade of 70 per cent, or qualify according to *Exception* noted above.

° The student must be fifteen years of age or older to receive Sunday school credit. Training Union credit on this book is not granted to Juniors and Intermediates.

2. *In Individual Study by Correspondence*

Those who for any reason wish to study the book without the guidance of a teacher will use one of the following methods:

(1) Write answers to the questions printed in the book, or

(2) Write a development of the chapter outlines.

In either case the student must read the book through.

Students may find profit in studying the text together, but where awards are requested, individual papers are required. Carbon copies or duplicates in any form cannot be accepted.

All written work done by such students on books for Sunday school credit should be sent to the state Sunday school secretary. All of such work done on books for Training Union credit should be sent to the state Training Union secretary.

III. This Book Gives Credit in Section I of the Sunday School Training Course